William Crossing

Amid Devonia's Alps

Wanderings and Adventures on Dartmoor

William Crossing

Amid Devonia's Alps
Wanderings and Adventures on Dartmoor

ISBN/EAN: 9783743408456

Manufactured in Europe, USA, Canada, Australia, Japa

Cover: Foto ©Andreas Hilbeck / pixelio.de

William Crossing

Amid Devonia's Alps

THE DEWERSTONE.

AMID DEVONIA'S ALPS;

OR,

Wanderings & Adventures on Dartmoor.

BY

WILLIAM CROSSING,

Author of "The Ancient Crosses of Dartmoor," etc.

" I seek thee, Nature, in thy wildest forms,
Thy mountain cataracts and frowning heights,
Where, as the unbroken prospect spreads around,
Life-giving breezes, health and spirits bless
The highland wanderer."—CARRINGTON.

Entered at Stationer's Hall.

London :

SIMPKIN, MARSHALL & Co., STATIONER'S HALL COURT.

Plymouth :

W. H. LUKE, PUBLISHER, 8, BEDFORD STREET.

1888.

PREFACE.

—◆—

THOUGH barren, in one sense, that district which is known as Dartmoor, in others, is now acknowledged to be rich indeed.

It possesses very much that is attractive beyond the "three remarkable things" of the old topographer of the seventeenth century. For the antiquary it is truly a happy hunting ground, and the lover of the wild and sublime in nature cannot possibly find in our island a grander field wherein to gratify his tastes.

I have been in the habit for some years of making notes of my researches on the moor, though prior to the year 1874 I made no systematic record of them, but since that time the results of my explorations have been carefully noted down. In the pages which follow, however, my design has not been to lay before the reader much of the fruit of these investigations, which are more particularly of an antiquarian nature, (though it is possible such may see the light of day at some future time) but to give a narration of the incidents of rambles on the moor, with brief descriptions of the principal objects of interest met with in their course.

It is only possible for me in the compass of a book like this to describe a few—a very few—of my wanderings, but I have culled from my note-books accounts of such as I consider fairly representative of my moorland peregrinations, and I sincerely hope that they may be found to be not devoid of interest, both for the general reader, as well as for such as have an acquaintance with the district of which my pages treat.

Splatton, South Brent, Devon.   W. C.

CONTENTS.

CHAPTER IX.

BY THE NORTH QUARTER COMMONS.

CHAPTER X.

AN ADVENTURE IN THE SNOW.

CHAPTER XI.

CRANMERE POOL.

APPENDIX.

AMID DEVONIA'S ALPS.

CHAPTER I.

A BRIEF CHAT ABOUT DARTMOOR.

SOME of the happiest days I have ever spent have been passed upon Dartmoor, and nothing now delights me more than a ramble over its solitary wastes.

As long as I can recollect anything at all, I can remember the old moor. In my childhood, no sooner did I pass beyond its borders, that

> " belt
> Of hills mysterious, shadowy,"

than I felt for it a love, and that love has increased with my years. Many months at a time have I passed upon it, and on the commons surrounding it, spending my days in becoming familiar with its rugged hills, (till at last I look upon them as old friends) and in learning what I could of its ancient stories from the dwellers in its confines.

While making this acquaintance with its tors, its streams, and its other natural features, I have not failed to carefully scrutinize the various objects of interest which it owes to the presence of man upon its hills

> " In the brave days of old."

I have made a thorough examination of its pre-historic monuments, such as stone circles, kistvaens, village enclosures, and the like. I have carefully inspected its streamworks and remains of ancient mining operations, its stone crosses, its curious old bridges, and searched out its partially obliterated and forgotten tracks. The descriptions of these objects of antiquity, with the measurements of them which I have taken, have been treasured up with care, their repository forming a storehouse from which I can draw with confidence in the accuracy of the contents. Nor have I omitted to jot down incidents connected with the moor which have come before me, and stories of its folk-lore I have eagerly seized upon and placed with the other matters which I have garnered.

My researches have not been confined to one particular part of the moor; I have explored it in all directions. The moor-men themselves do not know Dartmoor from end to end. With the neighbourhood surrounding the spot where they dwell and where their labours lie, they are perfectly acquainted, and many of them know, so to speak, every stone in their own district, but of those portions outside where their duties take them they are entirely ignorant. I know men—old men—who are now living in the southern portion of Dartmoor, having dwelt there all their lives, and being thoroughly conversant with it, who are yet entire strangers to the northern portion, and I am acquainted with those who, living in the north of the moor, have never seen the south part of it.

I remember some years ago talking with an old farmer who resided on the moor in the neighbourhood of Okehampton, and who in the course of our conversation, happened to say that he knew a good deal about Dartmoor. And about the immediate vicinity of his farm, I found that he certainly did, but when I came to speak of places at some distance off, he knew nothing of them, and in some cases had not even heard of them. He had never been to Post Bridge, (next to Princetown, the largest settlement on the moor) though he said one of his sons had once visited it; Hexworthy (a little settlement in the neighbourhood of Dartmeet) he knew not even by name; to Princetown he certainly had been—but only once—and yet he considered that he knew "a good deal about Dartmoor."

The forest of Dartmoor, which is the central portion of the moor, and defined principally by natural boundary marks, belongs to the Duchy of Cornwall and lies within the parish of Lydford, which, it is needless to say, is a very large one —I believe the largest in England. Very few of the inhabitants of this forest have ever seen their parish church. An old friend of mine, who was born on the moor, and has lived there all his life, can, however, boast that he has seen it twice, the first time being the occasion of his putting in the banns of marriage, and the second when he conveyed his bride there to go through the interesting ceremony. He has now sons, and grandsons who have nearly reached to man's estate, and though living ever since in the parish in which he was married, he has never from that day to this, again beheld the church. Not many years since I was up in the north quarter with one of the sons, and I pointed out to him Lydford church as the one in which his father and mother were married, and he is the only one of all the progeny that has seen it.

I would not, however, have my readers imagine that the Dartmoor people are heathens in consequence of this state of affairs. Far from it. There is a church at Princetown,

built by the French prisoners of war, at the commencement
of the present century; in 1868 a small mission chapel was
opened at Huccaby, near Hexworthy and Dartmeet, and in
the following year another of very similar construction was
opened at Post Bridge. Besides this there is the parish
church at Widecombe-in-the-moor, and at Princetown, Post
Bridge, and many little hamlets around the borders, there
are dissenting places of worship, so that the spiritual needs
of the dwellers on the moor cannot be said to be disregarded.

As many of the most interesting places in London are
neglected by, and unknown to, the cockney who has lived all
his days within the sound of Bow Bells, so there are many
spots on Dartmoor, which though having attained some
celebrity, the moor-men are personally unacquainted with.
I have taken men who have lived all their life on Dartmoor
to see Cranmere Pool. They had dwelt in the south
quarter, and never having had occasion to go " out auver,"
as they term it, the range of hills to the northward of the
Princetown and Moreton road, they knew nothing whatever
about that part of the country.

Dartmoor is, in fact, known in its entirety to but very
few. A moor-man of any particular quarter, who is riding
over it, perhaps, several days a week during summer, of
course, becomes in time thoroughly acquainted with that
ground. He knows every boggy place, each little path over
the hill-sides, by the rivers and through the new-takes, the
mining pits and rough places which he must avoid, the
fords which will enable him to cross the streams with ease,
in short, the particular features of the district he is quite
familiar with. But this quarter on which his avocations
confine him, is the only part of the moor with which he *is*
conversant. Ask him about places far removed, and he

will tell you he "doant knaw 'bout thackey; us never go out auver."

Nor will it be of much use to ask him about objects which it is not necessary for him to know in the pursuit of his calling. He seldom takes the trouble to examine these, and so heedlessly are they passed by that often he can scarcely tell you whether he has seen them or not. It may be that sometimes he can affirm, in reply to queries you may put to him regarding his knowledge of any particular object, that he certainly has "zeed un," but it is more than likely he will inform you at the same time that "us never doant think nothing 'bout such things."

But the Dartmoor man's love for his native hills, wild and rugged though they be, is very great. He is strongly attached to the old forest, and no spot in the "in-country" (as the cultivated land around the moor is termed) could be half so dear to him as the desert in which he was reared. As a Dartmoor farmer's wife once said to me when speaking of her husband's attachment to it, "Father 'll never leave it till he's carr'd away."

Dartmoor comprises portions of a number of parishes, though there is not one complete one upon it. The central portion of this great waste still continues to be a royal forest, and lies, as I have already remarked, within the parish of Lydford, and as that parish extends beyond the moor, a part only can be said to be on it, though, it is true, that is by far the greater part. The same observation applies to the moors or commons surrounding the forest, and which go to make up Dartmoor, (differing in appearance from the forest in no respect) for these moors belong to the parishes which lie around the confines, and there is consequently part of the parish on the moor and part not.

Most of these parishes which include a portion of Dartmoor within their bounds are what is known as venville parishes, —that is, parishes in which certain farms and tenements possess ancient rights of turbary and pasturage on the moor, termed venville rights, the occupiers of which were anciently supposed to be the king's special tenants, and were called venville men.

The limits of the forest are defined by certain boundaries —the marks with a few exceptions being natural ones—and there have been at various times perambulations made in order to define these bounds. It is divided into quarters, the north being the largest. The moors lying around it are divided from one another in the same manner as the forest is from them, that is to say, by natural boundaries, aided not infrequently by a granite post here and there. At the point where the boundary between two moors touches the line of the forest, there, of course, three parishes meet, Lydford always being one of them, and these points occur all around the imaginary line of the forest bounds, so that there are a number of points on Dartmoor where one by describing a small circle passes through three parishes. Some few of the moors dwindle down to rather narrow proportions as they approach the limits of the forest, the distance they are conterminous with it being short, but the parishes to which these moors belong all lie within venville.

The enclosed portion of Dartmoor is nearly in its centre, and may be roughly comprehended within the following boundaries : commencing at Rundle Stone* near Princetown the line runs to Merripit near Post Bridge, and from thence to Runnage, or Runnidge Farm on the Wellabrook, and so

---

* Or Rundle's Stone.

to Dartmeet, and back by way of Hexworthy, Swincombe and the White Works to Princetown.* But it must by no means be imagined that because this large tract is enclosed it is under cultivation. Those portions of it which really are so are of comparatively small extent, and it consists principally of parcels of moor divided by grey granite walls, forming enclosures into which cattle and sheep may be turned, when their owners do not desire them to go on to the open parts of the forest. These are called new-takes, and some of them are of considerable extent. Around the Dartmoor farms which are situated in this tract there are fields, and adjoining some of the most important, occasionally plantations of fir, but nowhere such an amount of cultivation as to materially change the natural aspect,—the soil and climate both forbidding that.

Surrounding this tract nothing may be seen but wild moor, untouched by any attempts at cultivation, extending for miles in every direction, but more particularly to the north and south. It is in these latter regions that the solitary and almost inaccessible spots lie, and of the two the north is the most extensive. The ponies which are reared on the moor, and roam in a semi-wild state over these portions of it, and the cattle and sheep which are pastured there in summer, are looked after by moor-men, whose especial business it is.

There are two main roads over Dartmoor, one leading from Plymouth to Exeter by way of Moreton Hampstead, and the other from Tavistock to Ashburton, and these intersect each other at Two Bridges, being also connected by

---

* The enclosed lands around Challacombe and Widecombe may be regarded as cultivated combes running up into the moor.

a road running from the Duchy Hotel to Rundle Stone, passing through Princetown, and in front of the prison gate. Strictly speaking these should be regarded as one main road running from Tavistock to Moreton with branches at Two Bridges to Plymouth and Ashburton, for such was the arrangement at the time of construction.

The road from Plymouth enters the moor at Peek Hill, above Dowsland Barn, and crossing Walkhampton Common passes within the forest limits immediately before reaching Princetown, the boundary being marked by a granite post, which may be observed on the right hand side of the way. From Princetown it descends the hill to the Blackabrook, which it crosses at the Ockerry Bridge, and goes on by the prison enclosures to Two Bridges, where the West Dart is crossed. After mounting the steep pinch behind the Inn it bears to the left under Crockern Tor, immediately on passing which the fine tor of Longaford on the range to the north becomes a conspicuous object. Soon Cherrybrook farm is passed on the left, and afterwards the Powder Mills on the same side, and a slight descent is made to New Bridge, —thrown over the stream from which the farm takes its name. Bellaford Tor lays at some short distance on the right, presenting a very striking outline. On gaining the bottom of the next hill Post Bridge is reached, and the East Dart passed over. The road lays through this little settlement, when the ascent of Merripit Hill is made, and in about another mile passing Statsbrook Bridge on the way, Newhouse—or as it is now called—the Warren House Inn, is gained. Immediately after passing this little wayside hostelry the bounds of the forest are crossed, and the commons which surround it entered upon once more. King's Oven lies on the rising ground to the left, and the lofty hill seen at some distance ahead, a little to the right, is Hameldon, a height from which a truly magnificent view is obtainable. Bennett's Cross, an old weather-beaten memorial of other times, will be observed on the common not far from the highway, and Vitifer Mine in the valley below. The road now passes on over the common, and leaves the moor at a place called Moor Gate, although no gate now exists there, and about four miles further on enters Moreton Hampstead, which is distant from Exeter twelve miles.

From Tavistock to Ashburton the road takes the following course. It leaves the town by Mount Tavy, and some distance further on the commons are gained, with Cocks Tor on the left. A magnificent view is here spread out before the tourist, with many a fine tor, and an extensive range of cultivated country. Descending the next hill Merivale Bridge, which spans the Walkham, is reached, where are a few cottages and a wayside house of entertainment known as the Dartmoor Inn. A fine view of Great Mistor is obtainable from near here, the height presenting a truly imposing appearance, its crown of rock towering towards the clouds. And now the road climbs up a very long hill to Rundle Stone, where the forest is entered, and descending on the opposite side, crosses the Blackabrook by a bridge about three quarters of a mile higher up the stream than the one thrown over it at the Ockerry. At a short distance beyond it passes the gate of Bair Down Farm, and descends to Two Bridges, joining the road from Plymouth to Moreton, but leaving it again on reaching the top of the steep slope behind the Inn, where it strikes off on the right. Skirting the enclosures of Prince Hall and passing over the Cherry-brook it goes on to Dunnabridge, where the noted drift pound is situated. A small stream runs down here, which

I well recollect when it was necessary to ford, but a bridge, built several years since, now carries the road over this little tributary of the Dart. That river is seen in the valley below on the right, as it comes down from the vale under Prince Hall. The next stream the road passes is Cock Lake, which is forded, and it then soon reaches Brimpts, near the entrance gate to which, a road turns down on the right hand, leading to Hexworthy, and over Holne Moor to Buckfastleigh and Ashburton. Passing Brimpts the road we have been noticing becomes for a short distance more of the nature of a Devonshire lane, with trees overhanging it, and ferns adorning the hedges. In summer the bare slopes of the moor are entirely shut out from view, and one can scarcely imagine he is on Dartmoor at all, so different in its characteristics does the scene appear. At the bottom is Dartmeet, a favourite place with excursionists, and one which will well repay a visit. A county bridge carries the road over the eastern branch of the Dart, immediatly above which are the remains of an ancient clapper bridge, which was unfortunately swept away in 1826, when the river was greatly swollen by rain during a violent thunder storm. These clapper bridges are formed of huge slabs of granite laid upon piers constructed of massive blocks of the same material, no mortar or cement of any kind being employed, and there are few more interesting objects to be seen on the moor. Below the bridge the West Dart comes foaming down from Huccaby Cleave to join its sister stream. The woods and plantations of Brimpts form a striking contrast to the rough hill on the opposite side of the valley, up which steep ascent the road now winds. The river here forms the forest boundary, so after passing over it the parish of Lydford is left behind, and the parish of Widecombe-in-the-Moor

ABOVE THE BRIDGE AT DARTMEET.

entered upon, which is very extensive, including a great part of Dartmoor within its area. On gaining the summit of the hill a grand view lays before the tourist, and the archæologist will find on the slopes around him numerous vestiges of ancient dwellings and enclosures. Passing on by Ouldsbroom Farm, the road runs through cultivated lands by Uppacot and Spitchwick Lodge to Pound's Gate, a moorland hamlet, where entering again on the commons it descends to New Bridge on the Dart, on crossing which the moor is left behind.

There are other roads on Dartmoor, but these two are the most important. There is one across Lee Moor, from Cornwood to Meavy, and between Tavistock and Okehampton the road passes over Black Down, which is a spur of Dartmoor. There is a road down through Challacombe under Hameldon, a portion of which has only been cut of recent years;—I remember having seen workmen engaged about it in 1874— one from Post Bridge to Runnage and over the Grendon Common ; and one by Bellaford and Pizwell in the same neighbourhood. Besides these there are roads on the commons to the east of the Widecombe Valley, and many smaller ones leading to some of the moor farms.

But if the reader will refer to a map of Dartmoor he will see that these roads leave entirely untouched the large tracts to which I have referred as lying to the north and south of that portion of the moor where the enclosures are situated ; and while many very interesting objects may be seen without diverging far from these roads, and an idea of Dartmoor be gained by traversing them, yet nothing can be learnt of those lonely regions without leaving the beaten track far behind. In these wild and desolate tracts nothing that denotes man's handiwork, except the scanty ruins of the huts of an ancient population, and vestiges of tin streaming operations, is to b; seen for many miles around. In the more inaccessible parts even these remains are scarce, and on many a broad stretch nature reigns supreme, the works of man never having intruded themselves in these inmost recesses.

It is possible to walk, pursuing a straight course, for a whole day, and never see a sign of recent occupancy or cultivation, or to meet with a single person on the journey. Nothing but great stretches of moor-land, rushing rivers, and lofty hills capped with fantastic granite tors can be seen, and it is difficult to realize that this rough and wild spot, where desolation holds its sway, is in the midst of the fairest county of England, and that immediately without its rocky barriers nature wears so different an aspect. But though the soft beauties of the lowlands of Devon are banished from this great granitic plateau, it possesses charms which belong to it alone, a grandeur by which the true lover of nature in its forms of wildness, and divested of the so-called adornments of man, cannot but be influenced and attracted.

And it is to this primeval region I would have the reader accompany me now; and if he will give me his attention while I detail some of my rambles over it, and allow me to detain him with such chats by the way as shall be necessary to give him some knowledge of the various objects passed by, I will promise him I will endeavour not to be tedious or dull. As for myself, I must own that as I am never tired of visiting the moor, so am I never weary of speaking of it. My wanderings over it I still continue, and my investigations I pursue with as much ardour as ever, always finding something fresh, and always experiencing delight in the search.

I know that I cannot expect to find all my readers equally enthusiastic with myself, but this I am quite sure of, that if such as at present are unacquainted with the grand old moor will but pay it a visit, they will not, if they have any soul for the romantic in nature, return from it disappointed.

CHAPTER II.

WALKHAMPTON COMMON AND PRINCETOWN.

THERE are few sweeter pleasures to be found than in re-visiting scenes which are endeared to us by early associations. Objects, the sight of which calls forth from the store-house of memory many a pleasing reminiscence, are welcomed as old friends, and cannot but exert a softening influence upon the mind. What joyous anticipations does the prospect of once more seeing these old familiar things create, and how eagerly do we look forward to sitting beneath the spreading tree in the spot so often chosen as our resting-place, to clamber again over the rocks on the hill-side half covered by the creeping plants, among which we often went in quest of the purple whortle-berry, or to stand by the well-known stile by the path which crosses the fields leading to the little cottage where dwelt the good dame to whose old-time stories we were never tired of listening. With what interest do we wander by the stream where in boyhood's days we angled for the sportive trout, or seek the wooded slope which we have often climbed, and where every little path was known to us, or look upon the rock-crowned hill afar off, to which in the long summer days we have wandered, and where many an hour has been spent in admiration of the glories around, or bend our gaze toward the slumbering little village in the valley, hid partially from view by the thick spreading foliage amid which the smoke is so gracefully curling. And should it be that these objects have been rendered more familiar to us in consequence of having been frequently re-visited since our first acquaintance with them, that cannot lessen their interest, for the recollections of those early days which cling around them never permit us to grow weary of seeking them again.

With thoughts such as these running through my mind I trotted merrily over Roborough Down, in the summer of the year of grace, 1866, on my way to the moor, bent upon a visit to some parts of Walkhampton Common and to Prince-town. It was a beautiful day, and the truly delightful panorama which spreads itself before the eyes of the traveller over this road was seen to its best advantage. I think it would be difficult to find a fairer view than that to be obtained from the down, looking towards Dartmoor. The fine chain of hills, of which Staple Tor and Great Mistor form the prominent points, is in full view; and North Hisworthy Tor, beyond which Princetown lies, with Sheepstor, more to the right, towering high above the vale where Meavy is seen nestling, are also conspicuous features in the landscape. Stretching part way up the sides of the hills, the cultivated country presents a striking contrast to their sombre slopes, the bright green fields, amid which are patches of woodland, with here and there a farm-stead, or village church tower, enlivening a scene which cannot fail to charm and attract the beholder.

Every step of the way was familiar to me, for I have known Roborough Down from my earliest childhood, and many a day have I spent wandering over it, and its precincts. I remember, although I was but a very young child at the time, walking one morning with my father from a cottage where we were then staying, to see a sham fight on the down, in which a fine body of Highlanders took part. Not long after the greater number of these poor fellows lost their lives in the Crimean war, the regiment embarking for the field from Plymouth.

On reaching the borders of the moor, I followed the high road up the ascent of Peek Hill, from the summit of which another grand view is obtainable. Near here is Lether Tor, a very interesting object, rising from the midst of a clatter of rocks, and nearer the high road is Sharp Tor. There are no less than five tors on Dartmoor by this name, a comparatively modern appellation bestowed on them in consequence of their conical shape. Here I struck off from the road over the common on my left in the direction of Leedon Tor, which is of an interesting character, and made my way down to the tram-road, on the line of which the present Princetown railway is constructed. This tram-road originally ran from Princetown, and the granite quarries near to that place, to the Laira above Cattedown, and in its course of about twenty-three miles passes through some exceedingly fine scenery. I have been very familiar with it from a boy, for a favourite ramble of mine was to follow it from Leigham tunnel through the woods to Bickleigh, and frequently, too, have I ridden over it on the empty waggons, between Clear-brook and the rock on Roborough Down. I have also ridden, early in the morning, from Peek Hill to Dowsland, when the waggons were laden with granite, and that portion of the line being on the incline, they ran down by their own weight, sweeping in their course around the very sharp turn on Yennadon, above the village of Meavy.

This railway was the proposal of Sir Thomas Tyrwhitt,

of Tor Royal, near Princetown, who having had the route surveyed, laid his plans before the Plymouth Chamber of Commerce, in the year 1818. The first act for it was passed in July, 1819, and the greatest part of it opened in September, 1823.

The details of Sir Thomas's propositions were published in a pamphlet entitled, *Substance of a Statement made to the Chamber of Commerce, Plymouth, on Tuesday, the 3rd Day of November, 1818, concerning the Formation of a Rail Road, from the Forest of Dartmoor to the Plymouth Lime Quarries, with Additional Observations, and a Plan of the intended line.* This pamphlet possesses an interest for all who are fond of matters pertaining to Dartmoor, but is certainly rather amusing in some parts, where the author shews himself to be exceedingly sanguine as to the benefits to be reaped from the construction of the line. Results have certainly not justified his expectations, although the rail-road proved to be very useful as a means of conveying the granite from the moor to Cattewater. Under the Fourth Head, Sir Thomas gives a list of Importable and Exportable commodities, which he ventured to believe would be conveyed over his line. The former consist of lime, sea sand, timber, slate, tiles, laths, coal, culm, groceries, wine, spirits, beer, porter, pottery, glass, furniture, &c., while the latter it is stated, would be granite in a multiplicity of forms, peat, mining products, flax and hemp, with their numerous fabrics, oil and oil-cake, potatoes and other vegetables; to which, the report says, may be subjoined, at a future period, wool, cloth, and skins. In the words of the pamphlet the formation of this rail-road would "gratify the lover of his country; reward the capitalist; promote agricultural, mechanic, and commercial arts; encourage home settlements; add a large quantity of improved land, strength, and population to the kingdom; and finally expand into a boundless field of speculation, *ever calling for fresh capital*, and ever yielding new incentives to industrious emulation, local prosperity, and public improvement." The italics are mine, and I feel very sure that this portion of the programme would most faithfully be carried out, if it should be attempted to "promote agricultural, mechanic, and commercial arts" on Dartmoor.

About the time when this pamphlet was issued there seems to have existed a kind of mania for cultivating the moor, and Sir Thomas, like many others of that day, evidently believed that such might be profitably accomplished, though it is difficult to understand how one with the knowledge of it that Sir Thomas must have possessed could have seriously imagined that it was possible to transform Dartmoor into an agricultural and manufacturing district. Thousands of its acres could never be cultivated at all, and the portion that it may be possible to reclaim, outside the few favoured spots that are already in the hands of the farmer, could not be brought under cultivation with any hope of profit. A number of speculators have set about what they termed "improving" the moor, but it cannot be said that any have achieved an unqualified success, while instances of failure are by no means scarce, heavy losses having not infrequently been made in these attempts.

There seems to be no doubt that the proper use to which to put Dartmoor is that of a grazing place for ponies, cattle and sheep, and employed in this way it becomes of very great service. A large number of cattle are pastured there annually, also sheep of the ordinary Devon kind, those of the Scotch breed remaining there all the year round, and

VIXEN TOR.

herds of ponies may always be seen roving at will over its wild steeps. Our forefathers were wise in this matter, for as a grazing ground was almost the only way in which they utilized the moor, making but very few attempts at cultivation.

As I made my way leisurely along the tram-road my attention was taken up by the view on my left hand, which was charming in the extreme. The valley of the Walkham was below me, and on the opposite side Pu Tor and Vixen Tor showed to great advantage, while beyond a most extensive prospect met the eye, with the Cornish hills in the distance. Enjoying this delightful picture I gradually approached King Tor, a very imposing pile of rocks, around which the tram-way made a considerable detour for the purpose of gradually ascending to the higher ground, the present railway following very nearly the same route. The line is carried along the slope of the hill, when winding around the majestic pile of granite, it is brought back on the opposite side, where it runs at no great distance from the section below it, having, however, after traversing so far, advanced but little towards its termination.

On one occasion a tram waggon laden with granite was in some manner accidentally started from the quarries, and commenced rushing down the incline with great speed before the workmen at hand were fully aware of what had happened. They gave chase, however, immediately they comprehended the nature of the mishap, but the runaway waggon had got too good a start for them to hope to overtake it. Fearing that it might do a great deal of damage they were anxious to stop it, and as it rushed rapidly on toward King Tor, they left the line, and running down the neck of land at their topmost speed gained it once more before the waggon came in sight around the hill. Hastily placing a block of granite across the rails, they were able to throw it off the line, and bring its career to a sudden termination.

The granite quarries are of some magnitude, a number of men being employed there, and the stone which is excavated is considered to be of excellent quality. The true lover of the moor, while fully realizing that works of this sort which afford employment for so many, are in themselves desirable, will, however, scarcely be able to help regretting that the face which it wore in the old time, is, around the scene of such operations, being entirely spoiled. Still, sentiment must bow before the welfare of the community, and after all Dartmoor is a big place, and we must not grudge to enterprise such a comparatively small portion of surface as such an undertaking needs.

The tram-road originally ran into Princetown, leaving North Hisworthy Tor to the left, (the present railway taking just the same route) but the rails over this portion of it have been taken up for many years, the expectations that "imports and exports" to and from Princetown would be carried over it, as I have stated, not having been realized, and the line was therefore used for little else than for transporting the granite from the quarries to Cattewater. This is now conveyed by the railway.

By the time I had reached the quarries, one of the mists which so frequently arise on the moor, came on, effectually shutting out the beautiful view I had been hitherto enjoying. Passing by the row of cottages erected for those connected with the quarry, I made my way towards Rundle Stone, and soon struck the road which I have described in the preceding chapter, and which leads across the moor from Tavistock to Ashburton.

My ride had up to this point been on that portion of the moor known as Walkhampton Common. This is of considerable extent and embraces within its boundaries a number of objects of great interest. There are many very fine tors, numerous remains of ancient mining operations, and a variety of prehistoric monuments. On the side where it is conterminous with the forest its bounds extend for a distance of six miles, and its average width from these bounds to the cultivated country is about three miles. Several streams take their rise within its area.

On arriving at Rundle Stone I had reached the forest bounds, which are mentioned on the Perambulation as extending from North Hisworthy Tor to Great Mistor, and the Rundle Stone forms an intermediate bond mark. The stone, which is seven feet in height, has the letter R cut in relief on its south-west face, near the top. Opposite to it, on the other side of the road is another stone, a much more modern one, not above half the height of the former, close by the wall, the part fronting the road being formed into an obtuse angle so as to present two faces, in the manner of an ordinary mile post. On the west side is the word *Walkhampton*, and on the easterly face *Lydford*, the parish, as stated in the former chapter, in which the forest lies.

Near Rundle Stone is a collection of quarrymen's huts, some of them the rudest habitations to be found on Dartmoor. Little tumble-down-looking cabins, built among the scattered granite of the moor, with small enclosures to them of nearly as dilapidated a character as the huts. Rundle Stone is about a mile from Princetown, to which place a road diverges at a short distance from it; on the north a large portion of the moor has now been enclosed by the convicts located at the prisons, and this tract reaches some distance up towards Great Mistor.

Turning my pony's head in the direction of Princetown I proceeded on my way thither, and passing by the prison gateway, constructed of immense blocks of granite, with the words "*Parcere Subjectis*" cut thereon, made my way to "mine inn," where my own wants and those of my little steed were soon attended to.

Princetown owes its existence to the prisons, which were erected for the reception of prisoners of war, at the suggestion of Sir Thomas Tyrwhitt, at the commencement of the present century, our country at that time being engaged in hostilities with France and America. Sir Thomas commenced his operations on the moor in the year 1785, and in 1798 built a residence, which he called Tor Royal. A farmer with whom I am acquainted, and who lives upon the moor, once told me that his father, who knew it long before Princetown or Tor Royal existed, was walking with a companion near South Hisworthy Tor, when they observed a heap of lime deposited, as if for building purposes. On enquiring about it they were informed that Sir Thomas was about to erect a dwelling, and soon on the spot where they had seen these evidences of contemplated operations, the walls of Tor Royal arose. Some few years after this Sir Thomas formed the idea that a site near his newly erected house would be a suitable one on which to build war prisons, such erections being considered desirable, as those at Plymouth, in which the prisoners were then confined, were inconveniently crowded. He laid his suggestions before the Government, with the result that in 1806 the first stone of the prisons was laid by him, the building, from plans by Mr. Alexander, being opened in 1808. As many as 10,000 prisoners were confined there at one time, which, of course, necessitated a large staff of officials to look after them, and to supply the wants of these, tradesmen settled around the great prison, and so in a very brief space of time a little town arose in the desert, which was named in honour of George, Prince of Wales, Princetown. In 1813 a little church, built by the prisoners, was opened, and this still serves for the inhabitants of the place.

Whether for the purpose of a war prison the site was wisely chosen, I cannot help thinking, is somewhat open to question. Had a due regard for the prisoners who were to be confined there been entertained, it certainly would never have been built. To place men who had been reared in the beautiful valleys of sunny France, as captives in a spot where the climate during winter is one of exceptional severity, seems like punishing them for taking up arms in their country's defence, whereas the only object should be their detention. There is a work entitled *La Prison de Dartmoor*, by L. Catel, and published in Paris, in 1847, which Mr. Davidson* characterises as "an absurd mixture of narrative, personal adventure, and the most improbable fiction," but says that it "bears traces of having been compiled either from the author's own experience or from the Journals of others who had been imprisoned at Dartmoor." Speaking of the moor M. Catel says "For seven months in the year it is a true Siberia, covered with unmelting snow. When the snows go away, the mists appear. Imagine the tyranny of perfidious Albion in sending human beings to such a place." While this is an exaggerated description of the inhospitableness of the Dartmoor climate, yet there is some portion of truth in it, and

---

* Bibliotheca Devoniensis.

the passage at all events serves to show the estimation in which the moor was held by Frenchmen.

For such of these who had relatives confined there, it is still a place possessing a certain kind of interest. I remember hearing my brother speak of a captain of a vessel, whom he met at Plymouth, some years ago, who was very anxious, on learning that he was so near Dartmoor, to know something of its situation and character, having, if I recollect rightly, known someone who had been imprisoned there.

The author of *Five Years Penal Servitude*, who was himself incarcerated at Princetown, since the prisons were turned into an establishment for convicts, in describing the place says : " Whoever first conceived the idea of confining Frenchmen in such a place must have been actuated by one of two very opposite motives. He must have either been instigated by a devilish but most refined cruelty to inflict on the enemies of his country, not only the punishment of man by imprisonment, but of nature too, in selecting a site with such a climate as Dartmoor. * * * * The other reason that induced the founder of the place to select such a site I think must have been a patriotic desire to save his native country from invasion. If Frenchmen, or any other foreigners, could only be led to think that the climate of England was all like Dartmoor, nothing would ever tempt them to invade such a country." This writer, however, states that Princetown is really a healthy place, and that it is so, is undeniable. A report by Sir George Magrath goes to show that the health of the prisoners was good, and in the bracing climate of Dartmoor it could not well be otherwise. In the respect of a healthy situation Sir Thomas Tyrwhitt was certainly not wrong in fixing on the spot he did, but why another, where health might have been equally as well preserved without the attendant discomforts which prisoners must have suffered in their confinement during the winters, could not have been fixed upon, 1 am at a loss to conjecture, unless it was that the dreamers of the time really believed that they were going to turn the old desert into a land flowing with milk and honey, and, by so doing, entirely alter its climate.

At the close of the war the gates were opened to the captives, and the prisons for a long time lay vacant. After being used for a manufacturing purpose—that of extracting naptha from peat—with the ill success that has almost invariably attended works of a like character on the moor, it was fitted up as a depôt for convicts in 1850, which purpose it still serves. Something of the sort was suggested in Sir Thomas's time, as in his pamphlet on the rail-road the possibility of such a course is mentioned. Many additions have been made to the buildings within the past fourteen or fifteen years, though all of them are within the walls of the old war prison. It is of a circular shape, and is said to be nearly a mile in circumference, standing on about thirty acres of ground.

When the prison lay untenanted, Princetown, finding its occupation gone, fell into a neglected and partially deserted state, but the establishment of the convict settlement has caused it to rise, Phœnix-like from its ashes, and become the place we see it to-day. Though, from its high situation it is, of course, subject to the buffetings of the storms of winter, it is a most desirable centre for the moorland tourist in the summer, and the best of accommodation may be obtained there. Now that the railway is extended to it, it is within easy reach from the outer world, though at the expense of one of its charms, that of utter remoteness.

The railway certainly seems an anomaly on Dartmoor, and though I must admit that it affords the means to many of seeing the moor who would otherwise be ignorant of its beauties, yet I cannot but agree with the remarks of a writer, who, in referring to this matter says : " Those who would wish to see Dartmoor by means of a railway, cannot wish to see Dartmoor in reality at all."* But this is an age of progress, and the iron horse will not be stayed. The railway, however, runs no further than over Walkhampton Common, reaching only to the forest bounds, and though, personally, I would much rather not have seen·Dartmoor desecrated by such an innovation, yet as I have used it myself sometimes, it seems rather like speaking ill of the bridge that has carried me over the stream, to decry it. Not to prove itself an exception to the generality of undertakings on Dartmoor, the railway fails to pay, and though true lovers of the moor may not greatly deplore this fact it is not to be supposed that there are any of such ungenerous disposition as to draw consolation from it.

How true it is that things are never so bad but that they might have been worse. What would the admirer of rugged and wild Dartmoor say to a railway running over its whole extent, and awakening the quiet repose of the forest with the shrill whistle of the engine ? Yet such was at one time contemplated, and actually considered feasible. I have before me as I write, a pamphlet containing a report of a survey made for such a railway by Mr. James M. Rendel,

---

* W. F. Collier. *Trans. Devon Assoc.* Vol. VIII.

the civil engineer, which was published at Plymouth in 1840.
To give some idea of how it was ruthlessly proposed to
destroy the beauties of the grand old moor, and carry into
its solitudes that which should never find a place there, I
will transcribe from the report the description of the route
it was proposed to follow. The projected line, the survey
of which was made in order to enable a company to apply
to Parliament for an act, was to commence at Pennycome-
quick, a suburb of Plymouth, and be carried by way of the
Houndscombe valley across the Devonport road near Man-
adon, and so on to Jump to the valley of the Plym; thence
through Meavy to Sheepstor Bridge, and so would enter
Dartmoor, and go on to Siward's, or Nun's Cross. "Over
Dartmoor, the line passes White-works Mine, down the
valley of the Swincombe river, across the West Dart river,
and through Prince Hall estate, into the Cherrybrook valley
at the bridge on the Tavistock and Moreton road—thence
down the valley which runs parallel with that road to near
Post Bridge, where it crosses the East Dart, and sweeping
round to the south of Merripit estate, enters the Runnage
valley near the farm-house of that name, and passing up the
valley, leaves Dartmoor by the Newhouse pass, near Vitifer
Mine." Meavy lies in a valley and Nun's Cross is on high
ground, and the curious enquirer may perhaps desire to
learn how it was proposed to ascend this steep gradient.
The distance, according to the report, is close upon five and
a half miles, and it was intended to draw the trains up by
means of ropes, the motive power to be supplied by two
water wheels, and a similar arrangement was to be adopted
on the other side of the moor for the purpose of pulling
them up from Chagford to the high ground near Newhouse,
in the vicinity of which there was to be a tunnel: there

was also to be one near Nun's Cross. On the portion of the line between these two points, that is to say, across the forest, the trains were to be drawn by locomotives.

In order to ensure a sufficient supply of water to work the wheels, large reservoirs were to be constructed on the moor by throwing dams across the Blackabrook valley, to the east of Princetown, another across the valley of the Cowsic, the stream that falls into the West Dart, just above Two Bridges, and a third across the East Dart valley, about three miles north of Post Bridge.

That the scheme never came to anything, all who are favourable to preserving from desecration a district which has been described as one of the most interesting in the British Isles, have reason to feel sincerely grateful.

On setting out from Princetown (the mist had by this time pretty well disappeared) I took the Plymouth road, and immediately on the outskirts passed the forest bounds once more, which are described in this part as running from South Hisworthy Tor to North Hisworthy Tor, (a row of granite posts, one of which, as I have mentioned in the preceding chapter, stands close to the road, marking the direction of the boundary line,) and re-entered upon Walkhampton Common. A short distance further on I passed the hollow known as Devil's Bridge, where one of the springs of the Mew takes its rise, not very far from the road. The immediate neighbourhood here is of a very interesting character, there being many remains of a bygone age scattered around. Below is an old stream work, and not very far off the dilapidated walls of a blowing-house—as such places were termed—where the miners used to smelt their tin, previously to conveying it to one of the Stannary towns to be

STONE CIRCLE, DARTMOOR.

stamped, according to the laws of the Stannaries of Devon. There are the ruins of many of these little buildings on the moor, hidden away among the combes, and in several of them are to be found stones with hollows cut in them, which it is likely were used as moulds into which the tin was cast. Around all are the remains of ancient mining operations, in very many cases of a most extensive character. At Stanlake, too, not far down the valley, are a pair of stone avenues, as they are termed,— and of which there are others on Dartmoor,—parallel rows of stones fixed in the ground, and extending for some distance, the space between them being some four or five feet in width. What purpose they served is still a matter of conjecture. Mr. Ferguson* considers it not unlikely that they were erected to commem- orate a battle between hostile tribes, and that the two rows represent the two forces. From other evidence we possess this does not seem improbable, although, as these avenues generally lead to a cairn, or kistvaen—the rude stone coffin of the Celts,—they may have been an expansion of the idea of the walled passage that sometimes led through the cairn to the spot where the body was deposited in its interior. In some cases the row consists of a single line of stones only, and one of this kind which we have on Dartmoor forms the longest pre-historic monument in the kingdom.

Near at hand, too, may be observed numerous hut circles, —the ruined foundations of the habitations of the ancient dwellers on the moor,—convincing us that this spot in the distant past was by no means so solitary as we find it now.

On Long Ash Hill, on this extensive common between

---

* Rude Stone Monuments.

Merivale Bridge and the row of cottages near the quarries, are also some exceedingly interesting remains, among them being some of the finest avenues on Dartmoor. There is also a very good specimen of the menhir, or long upright stone, and some of the hut circles are in a state of fine preservation.

Leaving Devil's Bridge I made my way over the road, and shortly drew near once more to Sharp Tor, passing which I descended Peek Hill, and soon after left the borders of the moor.

On reaching Dowsland Barn I turned aside to Walkhampton, in order to call at the smithy there, my pony Jack having cast a shoe; through lack of a smith I had been unable to have one put on at Princetown. Having had this necessary matter attended to I rode back to Roborough Down, where at the cottage of a good dame, a very old friend of mine, having known me from childhood, I stopped and rested for some time, and, with my appetite well sharpened by my ride over the breezy hills, did full justice to the homely fare which was set before me.

In the calm and quiet evening I again set out over the down, and after a pleasant ride reached the good old town of Plymouth.

CHAPTER III.

A RAINY DAY ON DARTMOOR.

IT was six o'clock on a dark November morning, and a drizzling shower was falling, causing everything without to assume a particularly cheerless aspect, when I was preparing to set out on a ramble over a portion of the south quarter of Dartmoor Forest. Not a very inviting day for such a purpose, I fancy I hear the reader exclaim, and so indeed I thought, as I looked out into the darkness; but I had made up my mind to go if possible, and would not allow myself to be discouraged because the weather happened to be rather unpropitious. Besides, I had always thought— and do so still—that a visit to Dartmoor on a rough winter's day, will repay him who is sufficiently undeterred by the state of the elements to make it. Though the bright summer time is naturally to be preferred in which to climb the heather-covered hills of the grand old moor, and one loves to seek it when the drowsy stillness of a summer morn is resting on all around, and the rivers and brooks are laughing in the sunshine, yet when its tors loom gloomy and sullen-looking on a dull and cheerless day there is about them something which powerfully attracts, a wierd appearance insensibly over-awing the beholder. When the mists float around them, half-shrouding and half-revealing their rocky summits, the effect is one which cannot fail to strike him, and when the snow covers the highlands, the dark peaks of the tors lifting themselves above it and contrasting with the dazzling whiteness around, there is a beauty inexpressible in the scene.

The time of the year never made much difference to me, and if it was not actually a stormy day, I have seldom deferred setting out when I have purposed "going to moor," and so on this particular morning when I looked out on the dull, sloppy weather, and could not help acknowledging to myself that it certainly was not exactly the kind to choose for a visit to Dartmoor, yet I did not feel any inclination to abandon my intended ramble. I looked instinctively towards the hills, but all was in darkness, so consoling myself with the reflection that when the daylight appeared the rain might probably cease, I completed my preparations for departure.

"It is raining rather much, isn't it, George?" I said to my man, when he made his appearance.

"Only a bit of a scad, sir," replied George, "it'll clear off soon."

Precisely : *only a bit of a scad :* the pride of the morning : just what I imagined : we shall have a fine day. Such were my thoughts on receiving this answer to my query.

How often do we find that men are ready to accept as true that which they desire to believe. That the wish is father to the thought is indeed no erroneous saying. Had I regarded the state of things with an unbiassed mind I must have known that there was little prospect of a fine day, and should have received George's reply with caution. Not that I had any reason to consider him a bad judge of the weather, but I ought to have guessed that there were certain influences at work with him which would have the effect of causing him to be over sanguine about the day proving fair. Now, I was going to take George with me, and I had promised him that we should run into Princetown before our return, and as he had never visited that place, and was anxious to do so, in order that he might get a sight of the "transports," as he termed the convicts, he was desirous that our ramble should not be put off.

We set out ere many of the good folks of Brent were yet stirring, having provided ourselves with a well-filled knapsack, for such is a very indispensable item when wandering on Dartmoor, and made for the moor-gate at Shipley, to which a walk of about a couple of miles brought us. Shipley Bridge is a very picturesque object, and the whole scene around is one that will be sure to attract the lover of nature. Being on the borders only of the moor, it possesses a mixture of wildness with the more softened beauties that cultivation presents. Above it the Avon (or Anne, as we always term it on the moor, and which is its more ancient appellation) comes tumbling down over a rocky channel, forming numerous cascades in its course, the aclivities on each side being crowned with a tor,—that above the eastern bank being Shipley Tor, and the one on the western side being Black Tor. The valley between them is very narrow, and they stand like fortresses of nature to guard the entrance to it. Granite blocks cover the slopes of the hills, amid which, especially on the side on which Shipley Tor is situated, the common fern, *Pteris aquilina*, grows in great profusion. At the foot of this hill, and not far from the bridge, is a little cottage, which adds to the picturesqueness of the scene. Below the bridge are fields enclosed within

walls of rough granite stones. the soil of which does not
seem to be of very different character from the moor itself,
while further down the vale others of a richer kind are
observable, the more favoured portions of nature here joining
the rocky enclosures on the skirts of the waste. The left
bank of the river below the bridge is clothed with thick
woods, which overhang and almost hide the stream from
view.

It was my intention to first visit Petre's Cross, which is
about three miles out from Shipley, and then go on to Aune
Head,* and with this intent we made our way up Zeal Hill,
the name of the aclivity on the west bank of the river. It
was now broad daylight, and the rain had ceased; so far
justifying George's assertion that the shower we had
experienced before starting was " only a bit of a scad. " but
yet appearances were not very promising of a fine day.
However, we endeavoured to persuade ourselves that Jupiter
Pluvius would favour us by withholding his downpour for a
time, and a few faint gleams of sunshine encouraged our
hopes.

Leaving on our left hand the old tram-road which was
constructed for the purpose of bringing in peat from
Red Lake Mires to Shipley Bridge, we pursued our course
straight up the hill, which is here remarkably free from
rocks or heather, and on the descent on the opposite side,
again struck it, and made it our track. This had always
been my route to Petre's Cross, for by following it, the rough
and at times boggy ground, which would have to be crossed

* Although I have used the ordinary name of *Avon* for the river, I
have not done so when speaking of its source, as that is never referred to,
on the moor or anywhere else, by any other appellation than *Aune* Head.

if a more direct way to the point in question is pursued, is avoided.

This tram-road, which at the date of the ramble I am now describing—the year 1872—was even then in a ruinous condition, was formerly laid with wooden rails, bolted down to blocks of granite sunk in the soil. The peat which was conveyed over it was subjected to a certain process for the purpose of extracting naptha from it, at the works erected near Shipley Bridge. The undertaking did not, however, prove a success, and on its abandonment the buildings soon fell into decay, in which state they remained for several years, but at about the time of which I am now writing they were in part renovated, and utilized by the Brent Moor Clay Company.* This after a short period of operations ceased to exist, and the buildings have again fallen into a dilapidated state. From Petre's Cross, which is not far from the terminus of the tram-road at the peat beds, there is a sharp descent all the way to Shipley, and the waggons ran down of themselves, horses being employed to draw them back when empty. An old man who was employed here when the works were in full operation told me, many years ago, that he had often known the breaks, on a frosty day, refuse to act, and had more than once seen the waggons precipitated through the roof of the buildings, the railway at its termination on the hill-side immediately above them being very steep indeed.

At Western Whitaburrow, the cairn on which Petre's Cross formerly stood, the men who used to work at the turf

---

* A Clay Company on Brent Moor was started some time previous to the one in question, and I believe the buildings were also made use of in connection with that.

cutting, built themselves a little house, using stone from the cairn for the purpose, such being necessary as there is no village, or suitable habitations, nearer than Brent, which is between five and six miles distant. These men were the destroyers of the old cross which was set up on the cairn, the shaft being all that is now left of it. The workman that I have referred to informed me that the labourers used to make incursions into Huntingdon Warren, which is in full view across the valley from Western Whitaburrow, and trap the rabbits, he having sometimes seen, he added with a smile of satisfaction, as many as a dozen being boiled at one time in the crock at the house on the cairn.

We reached this spot and made a halt for a short time to look around us. The weather so far, though rather dull, had not in any way interfered with the comfort of our ramble; one does not expect very bright sunshine in November, and as no rain had fallen since we had been on the moor we were getting on well enough. On a fine, clear day the view from Petre's Cross, as this spot is always called, is very extensive. On one side Hey Tor and Rippon Tor are observable, and in another direction Plymouth Sound, some fourteen miles off as the crow flies, between which two points a very great portion of the South Hams, as the southernmost portion of the county of Devon is termed, lies before the beholder. The tall chimneys of the works at the east end of Plymouth may be discerned, also the Hoe, and Staddon Heights. Looking over the long stretch of dark brown undulating heath to the north-west, a high hill may be seen rising in the distance. This is North Hisworthy Tor, the eminence close to Princetown, which I have referred to in the previous chapter, and to the right of it the grand outline of the frowning granite crest of Great Mistor is seen, and a long stretch of distant hills in the north quarter of the forest, with Fur Tor and Cosdon Beacon (the latter nearly seventeen miles off in a straight line) forming the background in this direction.

It was near Petre's Cross that in the preceding year (1871) an incident occurred which occasioned me a little excitement at the time. I had left Brent in the morning with my brother for a ride over the moor, taking with us two dogs, a very fine greyhound of his, and my spaniel Ranger. On nearing Petre's Cross, Hector, the greyhound, suddenly started a fox, and gave chase at a terrific pace, while we followed them as fast as the nature of the ground would permit us to ride. In a very short time the greyhound was close up to Master Reynard, who finding himself unable to distance his pursuer, turned round and stood at bay, shewing his teeth in a very threatening manner. The hound had done a deal of coursing in his day, but had, of course, never been accustomed to find his prey turn round upon him, and was naturally non-plussed, which the fox perceiving, off he started again, but only to run a few yards, with the hound close to his brush, when finding he could not shake him off, he once more turned and exposed his grinders to the astonished dog. This sort of thing was repeated several times, the fox rapidly gaining the top of the hill, while we were pushing after them in an endeavour to get close up. In our excitement and haste we were not very observable of the ground we were passing over, and all at once the horse on which my brother was mounted plunged into a boggy place, landing his rider safely on the turf in front of him. Impatient to see the result of the chase, he called out to me, who was just behind, to look after the floundering beast, while he set off after the hound on foot, running as swiftly as he could. We had, however, now lost sight of the chase, for Reynard had drawn the dog to the descent on the western side of Whitaburrow, and I judged he was making for Erme Pound, an old enclosure on the left bank of the Erme, where amid the scattered rocks near it he would have a chance of escaping from his pursuer. I dismounted, and succeeded in extricating the horse from the miry spot into which he had plunged, and which luckily was not very deep, and shortly after my brother returned, reporting that he had been unable to see anything of the fox or the hound.

We called the latter by name, but saw nothing of him for about twenty minutes, when he came running up towards us. We observed blood upon his jaws, but whether he succeeded in killing the fox or not, I cannot say. I think it very probable that Reynard dodged about, keeping the hound off by the determined stands which he made, until he reached the pound, where he would, no doubt, be able to gain some hole, and so escape from his enemy. He certainly deserved to for the plucky way in which he faced the hound when brought to bay. The spaniel took no part in the adventure, having been off in an opposite direction hunting on his own account, and saw nothing of the fox.

The pony which I rode that day had been quite a traveller; she had made the journey from London to the West of England by rail, by road, and by water. As an instance of longevity in animals, I may mention that she was thirty-four years old when she died, at the commencement of the present year. This good little animal, which belonged to a friend of mine resident in Brent, was reared by hand, her mother dying in a fit when the colt was but a few weeks old.

It is very necessary to exercise care in riding over Dartmoor in order to avoid the boggy spots that, even on what may be considered as fairly good ground, are frequently met with. Of course I am not supposing that anyone who understood at all what the moor was like would attempt to ride over the vast bogs that cover so much of its elevated parts, unless they were acquainted (as we who profess to be Dartmoor men are) with the tracks that in some instances cross them; but there are often, on ground which is otherwise safe enough, miry places where a horse may plunge in up to his girths, and hence the rider over Dartmoor cannot afford to be in any degree careless. But it is not always possible to avoid a mishap, and I have had more than one fall of this kind, as, I expect, have most who have been much over Dartmoor. I remember experiencing one on the day of the last meet of Mr. King's Roborough Harriers, some twenty years ago—I have forgotten the exact date—when we met at Hooe Meavy Bridge. A few days previously the hills had been covered with snow, and when we reached Ringmoor Down we found it lying in great patches, although not of any depth. When going at a good gallop over the moor (not, however, in chase of a hare at the time) the mare I was riding suddenly plunged into a soft place, a thin covering of snow preventing me from seeing it, and I was sent flying over her head. It must have been but a little spot, for I alighted on hard ground, and was up in a moment. On looking round for my steed I found she was half-way up her sides in the mire, and with a terrified look was beating wildly with her fore legs. I remember Mr. King shouting out to me from a distance " Whip her up; Whip her up ! " and taking hold of the reins I pulled her towards me, and with my hunting whip belaboured her hind quarters. Fortunately it was but a narrow strip of bog, and she was able to get her fore legs on the hard ground where I had fallen, and with a deal of struggling pulled herself out, almost covered with mud, with which I was also considerably bespattered. She was trembling violently, and it was some time before she recovered herself; I recollect I rode very cautiously all the rest of the day.

On another occasion a similar misadventure befel me, on the ground between a stream known as Dark Lake and the head waters of the Plym, where it is very boggy. There is some pretty good ground on one side of it, and by keeping to this the hill can be ridden over easily enough. But on the day in question a dense mist hung over the moor, rendering it quite impossible to see but a few yards around one, and I therefore could not choose my way so carefully as I could have wished, with the result that my pony plunging into the bog, flung me over his head in an instant. I was not alone, and my companion who was riding close behind me, at once dismounted and came to my assistance, and with his help we were able to put matters straight, though at first I was afraid it might have been an awkward affair, for I knew that, had we needed it, there was no help to be obtained within a circle of several miles.

Such mishaps are, of course, what everyone is liable to who rides on Dartmoor, whether he be well acquainted with it or not, but while this is so, it is none the less true that he who possesses a real knowledge of the moor, though he may occasionally meet with occurrences of the kind, is not likely to run into much danger.

I remember a circumstance which was related to me by a gentleman of my acquaintance which shows how necessary it is to know your ground before attempting to ride over it. He set out from near Two Bridges, accompanied by his daughter, with the intention of riding across the moor to Okehampton, that portion of Dartmoor being quite unknown to him! It is scarcely necessary to tell anyone who knows the district that he succeeded in getting but a very short distance on his journey. He endeavoured to follow the direction in which he knew the place lay that he desired to reach, and after a short ride gained the edge of the boggy land, or fen.* Not knowing the nature of it, it was not very long before his horse plumped down into it, and he found it imposssible to extricate him. His daughter who was following, luckily escaped, and conducting her to the safe ground they had lately left, he bade her ride to a tor that he pointed out, from which she would be able to see the houses at the powder works, to which she was to make her way with all speed and bring assistance.

The young lady set out upon this errand leaving her father to stand by his horse, which had sunk so deep in the bog that he could of himself do nothing towards getting the animal out, but she being unable to make her way to the tor alone returned once more to the spot. Seeing there was nothing for it, but to go himself for the required help, and as he could not allow his daughter to remain on the moor unprotected they were obliged to leave the horse alone, and set off "And never" said he, when he related the circumstance to me, "shall I forget the despairing cry which the

---

* The moor-men always pronounce this word *vin*, changing the f into v, and sharpening the vowel.

D

poor animal gave, when he found himself about to be deserted." After vainly struggling at first he had remained comparatively quiet while his master stood by, as if consoled by his presence, but when he saw him take his departure, that which we call instinct, but which is certainly divided by a very fine line from reason, caused him to feel his helplessness. However, his master was compelled to leave him, but hastened for assistance as speedily as possible, and returning with men and ropes, soon pulled him from his dangerous position.

In cases of this kind the moor-men always advise getting your horse on his side, if possible. While he is able to plunge, unless it happens that he can get his fore legs on hard ground, and so draw himself out, each plunge he makes only causes him to sink the deeper, and you have no chance of extricating him from the bog, except by the united force of several men, If, however, you can get him over on his side he becomes much more manageable, and may then be pulled from his perilous position with a vast deal more ease.

But I am detaining the reader all this time at Petre's Cross, and doubt not that he is anxious to get on, so craving his pardon for the delay we will at once on our journey.

We now entered upon the forest, Western Whitaburrow being one of its bounds, and left Brent Moor behind us. We took our way down the tram-road, which was carried from the point where we have been halting, to the place where the turf was dug—near Red Lake Mires—by a very sharp incline. At the distance of nearly half a mile from the summit of the hill, the tram-road is crossed by a very ancient moor-track, known as the Abbots' Way, but more frequently called by the moor-men Jobbers' Path. This track served as a means of communication between the abbeys of Buckland and Tavistock on one side of the moor, and that of Buckfast on the other. At the spot where the tram-road crosses it, and for a considerable distance on each side, and especially on the western, it is more plainly to be discerned than in any other part of its course. In many places only very faint traces of it are observable, and in others it is entirely obliterated.

Passing this old road, which as an ancient monks' path is truly interesting, we proceeded to the end of the tram-way, which is here cut down deep into the peat. Two wooden posts sunk into the ground mark the place where a press for the peat formerly stood, and at the time of which I am writing were connected with a cross-piece. We had now no longer any path, so striking over the boggy ground beyond the terminus of the old tram-road, we made our way to Heng Lake, a small rivulet which flows through a gully, where is an ancient tin work, into the Avon. The reader may look in vain for such a name as Heng Lake upon any map, or mention of it in any work on the moor, many which are mentioned by me being those of places known only to such as are acquainted with its more out of the way corners.

I here showed George a small wooden aqueduct—or launders, as such is locally termed—erected to convey water across this gully, and which I had seen in course of construction in the summer of the previous year. This water was taken in from the Avon close at hand, and conveyed along the sides of the hills to the clay pits on Brent Moor, for the purpose of washing the clay down to the works at Shipley. The now dry water-course may still be seen, but the launders have long since disappeared.

The lower part of Heng Lake gully is covered with remains of old tin streaming operations, so frequent on Dartmoor, but its higher part is boggy. The ground around its upper end is of the same nature, and on horseback, and during winter on foot as well, is in many parts impassable. From it, however, leads one of those paths which are made use of by moor-men in order to cross the miry portions of the moor. It runs to Green Hill, passing the head of Red Lake Mire. It consists of good hard ground, and it is possible to ride a horse over it with ease, while on each hand the ground is of a boggy, swampy nature. I know another by which one may ride over the miry ground that extends from the upper part of this same gully to the district of Anne Head, and which passes over the side of a high hill known as Caters Beam. Without these paths it would be utterly impossible for any four-footed animal to be taken over the swampy parts of the forest, and there are many places where, in winter, no one to whom they were unknown, could cross even on foot without danger. They are not very plainly to be discerned, and it is only to such as are thoroughly acquainted with Dartmoor that they are known at all, possessing none of the characteristics of beaten paths, but being merely strips of hard ground,—broken, perhaps, here and there,—amid the fen.

By those in the habit of passing much over Dartmoor on horseback, too high a value can scarcely be set upon these natural tracks, and the moor-man would frequently be obliged to make considerable detours were it not for their aid.

We had now reached the Avon just above a point in its course where it winds and twists among a number of rocks and boulders, and falls in numerous small cascades down into a wild and romantic hollow.

A rough wall, not seemingly so dilapidated as in an unfinished condition, runs on the left bank of the river, and is carried among the rocks in a curious fashion. This pertains to the enclosure of Huntingdon Warren, close to the higher part of which we now found ourselves. This portion of the forest was enclosed in 1808 by Mr. Michelmore, under a lease from the Duchy, and it continued in his family for upwards of seventy years. It is 789 acres in extent, and the ground was first taken in, I have been informed, as a new-take, a warren being afterwards formed on it. It seems well adapted for this, as it consists principally of a hill of good hard ground, with but few marshy spots on it. On one side it is bounded by the Western Wellabrook, a stream which also serves as the forest boundary from its source to where it mingles its waters with those of the Avon, and separates the parish of Lydford from those of Dean and Buckfastleigh. The Avon flows around other two sides of the hill, although the land included in the grant extends part way up the slope on the further side of this stream. The boundary is marked out on the northern side from the Wellabrook to the Avon by a kind of bank.

About forty yards below the rocks, over which it has been mentioned that this latter stream falls at the mouth of Heng Lake gully, and at the distance of thirty-five yards from the left bank, are the ruins of a small oblong erection, similar to others found in various parts of the moor. This was connected with mining operations, and is an old smelting—or, as it was termed, blowing—house. Its external dimensions are twenty-four feet six inches long, by fourteen feet nine inches wide, and in their thickest parts the walls have a breadth of two feet six inches. They are dilapidated in places, but where most perfect are about six feet in height. The doorway appears to have been in the side which faces the river.

In the north wall of this hut, but not quite in the centre, one stone three and a half feet long, and about nine inches thick, runs through it, (the wall having here a breadth of a little over two feet,) forming a sort of chimney breast. Under it an aperture like that of a fire place is formed, but on the outside where it is level with the ground, which is there much higher than in the interior. On this latter side the space is built up. This circumstance would seem to prove that an apartment,—possibly with a lean-to roof— formerly existed at this end, adjoining the main building. While searching around this curious little erection many years since I discovered a stone lying at a distance of thirteen feet from the doorway, which has two hollows sunk in it, not improbably moulds into which the smelted tin was poured. They are not, however, so clearly cut as others which I have discovered on the moor. Their shape is somewhat circular, and they are of a cup-like form; one measures seven inches across the top, and the other about six inches, and they are about three inches in depth. The stone in which they are cut is two feet in length, and one foot four inches in width.

The hut runs parallel to the river, in a north and south direction, and is built against the slope of the hill, which rises very steeply behind it.

On the side of this hill, and about a furlong to the eastward of the hut, is another but of very much smaller

proportions. Externally the walls measure fourteen feet in
length by eight feet in width, but the size of the hut
internally is only nine feet by four feet. In the manner of
many of these little buildings which I have examined, turf
is banked up against a portion of it on the outside. The
door-way is in the north-east corner, and in the south end is
the fire-place, which with the chimney in the wall, is in a
very complete state. Being considerably above the river a
wide prospect of moor is observable from this little hut.

Following the Avon we proceeded towards Cater's Beam,
a high round hill to the north. Our surroundings were now
of a very wild and solitary character. On our left a stretch
of boggy ground, looking gloomy and desolate, and beyond
which, though a good firm strip intervenes, are long reaches
of peat bog, extending to the further side of the head waters
of the Plym; on our right an expanse of heathy land, miry,
too, in some places, with Ryder's Hill forming the background, and before us the eminence towards which we were
making our way.

Passing another stream work (for these remains of the
old mining on Dartmoor are most numerous) and still
keeping to the banks of the river, we soon reached Fish
Lake, a small tributary of the Avon, draining from the
midst of bogs. Immediately above the confluence, scattered
heaps of stones, very much overgrown with vegetation, will
show the explorer of this remote part of the forest, that the
ancient miner has also been at work here. Two little huts,
which may be seen at the distance of about a score or two of
yards from the left bank of the Avon, are worth describing.
They were probably places of shelter, and for the keeping of
the miners' tools. They are quite close together, and the

passage way between them, I think it very likely, was
covered in, so that they in reality formed two apartments in
one building. The northern one, which is the smaller, is
banked up on the outside with turf, and is somewhat of a
circular form, measuring thirty-eight feet in circumference.
Internally, however, the apartment is of a different shape,
not precisely square, being built in a form approaching that
of a wedge, and its area is only a few feet, so much of the
ground being taken up by the wall and bank of earth. The
doorway is in the middle of the passage that runs between
the two, and faces that of the second hut. It is only about
fifteen inches wide, and has one side formed of a single
upright stone, and the other built in a wall-like form.

The other hut is of an oblong shape, measuring on the
inside eleven feet by nine and a half feet. The side farthest
from the river is built close against the rising bank, and the
south end is covered by a slope of turf which is raised against it.

The space between the two buildings is just sufficiently
wide for a person to pass.

These evidences of former industry in a spot so secluded
and remote are well worth examination by the curious
explorer of the moor.

By this time the sky looked more threatening, and I began
to be doubtful whether the " bit of a scad " of the early
morning was not going to be followed up by something that
we should be compelled to take more heed of. We pushed
on, however, keeping along the foot of Cater's Beam, close
to the river's bank, where the ground is good ; in winter the
hill itself is little else than bog. We were now very near
the source of the stream, which takes its rise in an extensive
morass, the most dangerous in the south quarter of

Dartmoor. Formerly Fox Tor Mire was considered the worst spot, but the mining operations at the White Works partially drained it, and it is now not nearly in so boggy a condition as at one time. Cattle have frequently been lost in the mire at Aune Head, and I remember seeing old John Bishop of Swincombe, in the summer of 1879, cutting a trench in it, for the purpose of draining it somewhat, if possible, the farmers who were in the habit of pasturing cattle on that quarter of the forest being desirous of seeing whether it could not be rendered less dangerous. This did not seem to be very effective, however, for it was not long before it became choked up with bog again, and the traces of it nearly obliterated.

We had now (about ten o'clock) reached a part of this morass which is known to the moor people as Little Aune, a bog from which drains a dull sluggish stream, at right angles to the main one. Aune Head itself is at some little distance above this, but from the one to the other there is nothing but a stretch of morass. As we proceeded along the edge of this, the sky became more overcast, and the air was sharp and cold. Large flakes of snow began to fall, and deeming it prudent to seek some shelter, we made for a dry gully, where laying ourselves down on the windward side, we opened our knapsack, and ate a hearty lunch, sheltered by an overhanging bank from the now fast falling snow. Not over comfortable conditions, perhaps, on which to partake of a meal; but the wanderer on Dartmoor must not be too particular about matters such as these.

The fountain-head of the Avon was just below us, and is one of the most curious to be seen on the moor, for though situated in the very midst of the mire, and in a seemingly unapproachable spot, is nevertheless to be very easily reached. The stream, which is here but a mere rivulet, has a hard gravelly bottom, with firm banks to it, the latter forming a strip of hard ground running out into the mire. The head of the stream consists of a little pool, or basin, and the water flowing over on one side of it, a tiny rill is formed, and this rill is the Avon.

In its course to Shipley Bridge this river receives several tributary streams, its waters being augmented, as we have seen, by Fish Lake and Heng Lake, ere it has advanced far upon its course. Below the rocky hollow where it receives the latter small stream, it flows through a narrow valley, the warren being on either hand. Lower down the valley becomes wider, and the river makes a bend to the left, but before doing so sweeps beneath a rude bridge formed of granite slabs, not, however, an ancient one, although constructed on the plan of them, but having been erected I have been informed, by Mr. Michelmore, the encloser of the warren. Below this, close to Huntingdon Corner, another small stream, flowing down from Bush Meads, mingles its waters with the river, whose course is then to Lower Huntingdon Corner, where it is joined by the Western Wellabrook, Huntingdon Cross, a very complete, though small, example of the ancient stone crosses of the moor, standing but a few yards from the confluence of the two streams

Here the Avon leaves the forest, and becomes the boundary between Brent and Dean Moors, and flowing onward over its rocky channel is joined a little further down by the stream which flows from Brockhill Mire. In this part of its course it flows by numerous remains of a bygone age, some fine specimens of ancient British villages being situated on both its banks, as well as vestiges of medieval mining operations. Many little rivulets pour their tribute to swell its volume, one falling into it at the point where it leaves Dean Moor, and enters entirely on Brent Moor. After passing between Black Tor and Shipley Tor, it reaches Shipley Bridge, as has been already described, and immediately below this it bids adieu to the moor.

A few hundred yards further down are Zeal Pool and Cascades, which with their surroundings form one of the most romantic pictures to be seen on the borderland of Dartmoor. The best point from which to view the cascades is from above the head of the pool, where it is necessary to get down on to the rocks close to the stream, as the river here is almost concealed by thick and tangled foliage. These waterfalls extend for some distance, the stream tumbling over innumerable ledges of rock in sheets of glistening spray. At the bottom of the last cataract, the spot which I have spoken of as being the best to view them from, they foam amid the rocks for a short distance, when they suddenly leap out into a yawning cañon, deep and dark, at the bottom of which, their wild impetuosity now restrained, they glide sullenly along in their narrow channel, between perpendicular walls of solid rock, which re-echo the roar of the falling waters above. So deep and shrouded is this hollow that the bright sunshine fails to penetrate it sufficiently to enlighten its gloom. The Avon slowly makes its way along it, until at length the walls of rock recede and the stream flashes forth into the daylight once more. The spot is but little known, but a visit to it will well repay the lover of the romantic in nature.

Below Zeal Pool the Avon receives the waters of the Red Brook, which fall into it over a ledge of rocks a few feet in height, and flows onward through a deep valley to the little market town of South Brent, Avonwick, Diptford, Loddiswell, and Aveton Gifford, below which it mingles its waters with the sea.

The snow which fell in large flakes for some little time gradually changed to a misty rain, and there seemed to be no prospect of an immediate improvement. However, as I had made up my mind for a day's ramble, I did not care to go back, so with hopes that the weather might yet clear, I prepared to go forward once more. Leaving Aune Head Mire, which though on high ground, lies in a kind of hollow, we struck out over the ridge in the direction of the Swincombe valley.

Had the day been clear the view would now have been a most attractive one, for soon after leaving the swamp the summit of the ridge is reached, and an exceedingly fine prospect is opened up of the central portion of Dartmoor, which it will be readily observed is the least elevated of the whole of this great granitic plateau, and where nearly all that is enclosed of Dartmoor is situated. But the misty weather entirely prevented our seeing anything of it then, and the only objects we got a glimpse of as we descended the slope of Terhill, as the hill on which we now were is known on the moor, were Fox Tor, with the White Works beyond, when once the mist lifted for a few moments.

The Swincombe river rises in Fox Tor Mire and pursuing an easterly course for about three and a half miles flows into the West Dart at Sherburton Firs. On reaching the stream, which we did at somewhere near the middle of its

course, after a walk of about a mile and a half from Aune
Head, we selected one of the numerous crossing places formed
by the rocks in its channel and on gaining the opposite bank
proceeded in the direction of Moorlands, across the corner
of Tor Royal New-take, an exceedingly large enclosure, over
which a green track leads from Swincombe to Tor Royal and
Princetown.

By this time the mist had lifted in a great measure,
but the rain descended in torrents. I told George that
there was now no hope whatever of his seeing the
"transports", for in such weather as that they would all be
within the prison walls, but we determined that we would
still take in Princetown nevertheless, before we went back.
Nothing daunted by the rain, therefore, we kept on our way;
it was "in for a penny, in for a pound", and as we could
not possibly get much wetter, I decided not to curtail my
proposed ramble. We soon reached Moorlands, from which
a road leads to a bridge over the West Dart, just in front of
Prince Hall. This we followed, and in summer time truly
delightful is the vale it runs through. The road descends
to the bridge having on the left hand a plantation, with an
undergrowth of ferns and other plants, while in front the
enclosures of Prince Hall rise from the opposite bank of the
river, presenting a striking contrast to the wild surroundings.
The channel of the Dart is here rather wide, and an
exceedingly fine view of it is to be obtained from the bridge,
but the weather would not permit us to stay to observe any
of this, so we made our way up the ascent in front of Prince
Hall.

This estate is one of the ancient tenements of the forest,
and at the close of the last century was acquired by a Mr.

Gullet, who set about making great "improvements" upon it, and erected numerous outbuildings. From him it was purchased by Sir Francis Buller, who made great additions to the residence, and also enclosed a large quantity of ground and planted as many as 40,000 trees upon it. Mr. G. W. Fowler, of Liverpool, took Prince Hall in 1846, and expended a good deal of capital upon it, but with no successful financial result. The farm buildings are erected upon a very fine scale, and the moor people jokingly say that the only thing wanting to make them complete is a cider pound. As there are, of course, no apples on Dartmoor, such would be worse than useless, and this is only spoken in ironical allusion to the style and plan of the buildings, which are constructed in the manner one might expect to see upon an estate in a flourishing agricultural district, and seem designed for purposes for which they are not likely to be required on Dartmoor.

I well remember the time when Mr. Fowler relinquished the estate, although I was very young then, as it was more than thirty years ago. My father, who was acquainted with him, received an invitation to dine with him a day or so previous to his leaving, and set out to drive from Plymouth. The morning was fair, but the day did not fufil its early promises. When less than half way on the journey, a thunder-storm arose, with torrents of rain, which continued for some hours. My father reached Dowsland Barn, but found it impossible to proceed further, so was obliged to take shelter until the storm moderated, by which time it was too late for him to proceed.

Passing the farm buildings we gained the drive leading to the high road that crosses the moor, where there is a lodge. The low trees planted by the side of this drive are all bent forward in an easterly direction, showing the great prevalence of westerly winds on the moor. On reaching the main road that leads from Ashburton to Tavistock, and whose course I have sketched in my first chapter, we turned in the direction of Two Bridges. The rain still continued to pour down in torrents, and we were not sorry to seek the shelter of the inn there—the Saracen's Head, (I have always thought that the Druid's Head would have been a far more appropriate sign) but as the rain showed no signs of abating, and there was nothing to be gained by waiting, out into it we went once more, and bent our steps to Princetown.

About mid-way between the two places the road is carried over the Blackabrook by a modern bridge, and immediately below this is an ancient clapper bridge of two openings, and though much smaller than some others on the moor, is a very good specimen of these erections, being in a remarkably fine state of preservation. There are small parapets to it now, but these are modern additions. A cottage built somewhat in the style of a Swiss chalêt (at that time an open balcony with verandah surrounded it, but this has since been removed) stands close to the old bridge on the right bank of the stream, and is known as the Ockerry. During the time the French prisoners of war were confined at Princetown, two generals on parole named Rochambeau and Boyer lived at this house.

On reaching Princetown we found the place looking desolate indeed. The incessant downpour prevented anyone from making their appearance in its street, all the inhabitants keeping within doors, which good example we hastened to

follow, turning into the Duchy Hotel, where we took shelter
for an hour. Here we also fortified the inner man, previous
to resuming our journey, for we had still a walk of over
twelve miles between us and Brent, about ten of them being
across the moor. We felt rather disinclined to leave the
cheerful fireside of that comfortable house of entertainment,
especially as the rain had not abated in the least, but not
wishing to be home late, I felt that it would not do to linger
too long.

On setting out we took the turning by the side of the
Railway Inn, and made our way through the rain to South
Hisworthy Tor—Look Out Tor, as it is generally called in
the neighbourhood—and from thence pushed on to Siward's
Cross. It was now misty, although not very dense, so that
we could see a fair distance around us, and we plodded on
as cheerfully as we could under the circumstances. The
wind was blowing the rain in our faces, but we stepped out
endeavouring to treat it as a light matter, though it certainly
required some amount of self deception to do it, for we were
having a taste of real Dartmoor weather.

Arrived at Siward's Cross, or as it is more often called,
Nun's Cross, we stopped for a few minutes to look in upon
the farmer there, who at that time was but a recent settler,
having been there only about two years. He had taken in
some land and built himself a small house, where he still
makes himself comfortable enough, and can certainly be
under no apprehension of being annoyed by troublesome
neighbours. Siward's Cross is a very fine example of these
venerable objects, and is mentioned in a perambulation of the
forest made in 1240. Its shaft is unfortunately broken, but
the damage has been repaired as far as possible by iron

clamps, so that in appearance the old cross has suffered but little.

Wishing Mr. Hooper, the farmer at Nun's Cross, farewell, we ascended the hill to the southward, and hastening on again through the mist and the rain which on the summit beat in full fury against us, soon commenced the descent on the opposite side. The ground was in a plashy condition, being thoroughly soaked with water, rendering walking a far from comfortable exercise. At the foot of the ridge over which we had now come runs the Plym, which we crossed not very far from its source. The hill on the other side of this stream, and which now lay before us, is known to the moor-men as Crane Hill, and is very boggy in some places. It was on the side of this that I plumped with my pony into the bog, when riding in the mist, as I have mentioned, but that was farther out on the forest than where we now were. Keeping on the side of the hill where there is hard ground, and thus avoiding the bogs, we toiled upward, the weather in no wise abating till we reached the summit, when it improved a little,—but only a little,—and for a very short time. The mist lifted, too, for a small space, enabling us just dimly to perceive at some distance on our right, (for the day was getting spent,) the pole which at that time was fixed by the side of Broad Rock, an object well known to the moor-men, situated on the verge of the Abbots' Way, and not very far from Erme Head.

Crossing Dark Lake, a tributary of the Erme, we continued on our way, but not at such good speed as we had been able to make in the morning. We had traversed a good many miles, and for several hours past in a perfect

E

deluge of rain. This was now telling upon us, and we began to feel rather weary. However, we had still several miles of moor to get over before reaching Shipley Bridge, and it was of no use giving way to any feelings of this sort, so we held on. Soon the stream that runs down from Middle Mires on Green Hill was reached, and our next point was Red Lake Ford, where we should strike the Abbots' Way, and so have a track to the old tram-road near Petre's Cross, which we had passed over in the morning.

By the time we arrived at the ford it was dark, and still raining as heavily as ever. For some while we had both of us been feeling exceedingly hungry, and I more than once had pictured in my mind the cheerful fire at home, and the well laden board which I knew was awaiting me there, and regretted that we had not a further supply of food with us to supply present wants. Plodding along up the Abbots' Way, through the darkness, with the rain beating straight in our faces, and conversation being impossible, I commenced turning over in my mind the events of the day. Feeling nearly famished it is perhaps scarcely to be wondered at that my thoughts turned to the occasions on which we had rested and partaken of food during our journey, and that I could not repress a wish that we had now one of the substantial pasties with which the knapsack had been furnished in the morning. How acceptable it would be, I thought, and how much better some food would enable us to get over the remaining half dozen miles that lay between us and home. My reflections continued in this strain when suddenly it struck me that after all there must be one of the pasties still remaining in the knapsack, though as we had considered that all had been consumed, I feared lest I might be mistaken. I knew the number I had brought away from home and in running over the occasions upon which we had helped ourselves to them, there was one which I could not account for. George was carrying the knapsack, and was some few yards ahead of me, so with a hope that I might not be disappointed, I called upon him to stop, which he did, and putting my hand without loss of time into the knapsack, there, sure enough, buried among several other items, was the pasty. To exhibit it to the delighted George, for he was none the less pleased at the discovery than myself, and to divide it with my knife, occupied but a moment, and we stepped out through the darkness, making the acceptable morsel quickly disappear.

Drenched and soaked with the rain we gained the old tram-road, which now became our track, but of course in an opposite direction to that we had pursued in the morning. On reaching Western Whitaburrow the worst of our journey was over, for though we had still about five miles to walk, more than half of this—from the cairn to Shipley—is mostly down hill. We were not long in covering this distance, and with the rain still descending in torrents, and the thick darkness rendering everything invisible, we at length reached home, none the worse for our day's soaking on the moor.

CHAPTER IV.

A LONG TRAMP.

IN the summer of the year 1874, a friend of mine was staying with some relatives who resided for a short time at Brent, and never having visited the moor, expressed to me a desire to do so, and we therefore decided upon a ramble together over its breezy hills.

It was the month of August, and the weather was all that could be desired for such a purpose, and as I was bent upon showing my friend as much of Dartmoor as was possible in a day's ramble, I proposed that we should set out at daybreak, so as to have plenty of time before us.

The evening previous to the day on which we had arranged to make our excursion I spent at the house of my friend H——'s father, and having to rise betimes in the morning, I had not intended staying very late. But, alas, for my resolves! The company was so agreeable that very soon all thought about the morning had vanished, and the hours flew so rapidly that ere we were aware of it midnight had slipped by.

" Well, there won't be much sleep for us if we are to start according to my original intention," I said to myself, " but two or three hours will be better than none," and as I had given directions to be called, and also that my man was to go to my friend's house and arouse him as well, I decided that we ought to seek our couches—*vulgo,* go to bed— without more delay.

We were a merry little party, and "There's time enough yet," and "You don't want to start at such an unearthly hour," were the answers to my suggestions that it was time for me to be off, if we were to have any sleep at all, and H——'s father—good kind-hearted old man, I shall always revere his memory—joined in with his favourite expression, "Time was made for slaves," and insisted that I must not think of going yet. I looked at H——. Should we postpone our departure till after breakfast, or should we get some rest now, and start according to our plans! He was in favour of setting out early, but was not perfectly clear as to the possibility of such a course, considering it morally certain that if we once got to bed the sun would be very high in the heavens before we should experience any inclination of quitting it again.

In this state of uncertainty we were, when—happy thought—here was a solution of our difficulty—*why go to bed at all?* Why break up the little party? We could go on enjoying ourselves for another hour or so, and then see about starting. We troubled no more about the matter, but decided upon this course at once;—not a very wise one, certainly, but it commended itself to us then, and we followed it.

Before setting out we refreshed ourselves with some good, strong coffee, and while yet it wanted some time ere the day would break, we started on our journey, with the stars

shining brightly, and every promise of a fine day. Soon
these twinkling lamps of the sky began to pale, and as we
neared the moor the faint flush of the coming dawn was
observable. On reaching Shipley Bridge, instead of mounting Zeal Hill, as described in the previous chapter, we
followed the road that runs for a short distance by the
river side, and very soon passed through the gate of Brent
Moor Villa. Just inside this, on a ledge of rock, amid the
shrubs which have been planted here, and which in this
sheltered hollow flourish so luxuriantly, a small pedestal of
granite is observable. It was erected by the late proprietor
of the villa, in memory of his little daughter, and inscribed
upon it are the following touching lines.

M. M.

March 27th. 1863

My lovely little Lily
   Thou wert gathered very soon,
In the fresh and dewy morning,
   Not in the glare of noon.
The Saviour sent His angels
   To bear thee hence my own,
And they'll plant thee in that garden
   Where decay is never known.

Shortly after passing the grounds, which are entirely
surrounded by moor, we crossed the Avon, and pursued our
way along its eastern bank, passing the old disused granite
quarry, near the banks of the stream. The ground is here
firm and good, and the hollow through which the river runs
is very secluded, and of a pleasing character. A little way
up the stream we halted, and partook of some refreshments.
The sun was just rising, gilding the hill tops. diffusing a
warm glow around. Everything near us, but the rippling

river at our feet, was calm and still, and that quiet, almost
inexpressible feeling, which is only to be experienced at the
dawning of a summer's morn upon the moorlands, stole over
us. How peaceful was the old moor ; what a contrast to the
turmoil of the busy city, where men toil all day long in the
pursuit of wealth, and in doing so too often sacrifice the
pure joys which are offered them with a free hand in the
beautiful country. We revelled to the full in the enjoyment
of the delightful scene, and in the fresh breezes of the rosy
dawn, and as the sun rose higher and higher, and cast its
beams full upon us, we proceeded on our way up the valley.

Here I pointed out to my friend the ruins of an ancient
British settlement, the basement walls of the huts erected in
a far-off day showing where the hardy sons of the wilderness
had made their home, and further on Huntingdon Cross,
which, as I have already mentioned, stands near the
confluence of the Western Wellabrook with the Avon, and
forms an interesting object in this secluded part of the moor.

Leaving the Avon and following the first-named stream,
we made our way to Huntingdon Warren House, and calling
in were welcomed in true Dartmoor fashion, and pressed to
partake of some homely cheer. It was now close upon
seven o'clock, and the morning hitherto so bright and fair
became thickly overcast, and a dense mist arose obscuring
everything from view. We stayed at the warren house for
some time, and looked at a very good collection of mineral
specimens which had been found in various parts of the
moor, and chatted about divers matters pertaining to
" old Dartymoor." Our hopes that the mist would lift,
and that we should again enjoy the bright and beautiful
sunshine, seemed doomed to disappointment, for the

impenetrable curtain hung over everything around, rendering
objects at the distance of a score or so of yards quite
invisible.

As we looked out from the windows of the warren house
upon this prospect it did not seem very cheering, but no good
could be done by repining, so with the resignation of true
philosophers we bade our entertainers farewell, and stepped
out into the uninviting weather. I was bound first for
Aune Head, as I wished H——, to see the source of this
stream, so on leaving the house I passed up through the
warren, having the Wellabrook on my right hand, until I
reached some ancient mine workings, which H—— was
interested in examining. From here, instead of making
straight for Aune Head, the intervening ground not being
the best to travel over, especially in the mist, I pursued a
course by which I struck the river below Fish Lake, and we
then followed it to its source.

All this time we were able to see but a very few yards
around us, which, while it was not particularly pleasant, yet
afforded my friend an opportunity of seeing what a real
Dartmoor mist was like. Crossing Sandyway, an old track
which passes the upper part of Aune Head Mire, we
proceeded over the crest of the hill towards the valley of
the Wobrook, and on our way I was able to point out to
H—— some turf-ties, and numerous piles of peat loosely
stacked for the purpose of drying, preparatory to being taken
in to the farms and stored for the winter. The Dartmoor
farmer need never want for fuel, for peat is in abundance to
be obtained on the moor. Each farmer has his own particular place where he cuts it, which is termed a turf-tie.
Peat cutting is by no means easy work, especially when the

soil, as is so frequently the case near the surface, is full of the roots of the heather; at the distance of a few feet below the surface it is, however, not so difficult to cut, and the peat is of better quality. An instrument specially adapted for the work is used, and to cut a length of forty yards, of the width of two slabs of peat,—or, as it is called, *two turves wide*,—is termed a *journey*, and for a practised hand to cut a journey and a half is considered a very good day's work. The surface turf, by a rule of the Duchy, must be replaced in the tie, so that the pasturage be not interfered with.

Formerly it was used in all farm houses on the borders of the moor, but many of these now being within easy distance of railways, coal is more generally employed, but on the moor itself no other fuel than peat is used. In some places it is of a very great depth, borings having shewn that from twenty to thirty feet of it are resting on the gravels. Speaking once to a moor farmer of the great advantage it was to them, I was rather amused at the view he took of the matter. "Ees," he said, " 'tis wisely ordered that us should have turve 'pon the moor. 'Tis my belief 'twas washed up by the Vlid (Flood) cos 'twas knawed us couldn' get no coals out here!"

Striking into the top of Hooten Wheals, the name of a gully where is an extensive stream work, and which name may possibly be a corruption of Wooden Wheels, we descended to the Wobrook, and crossing it gained a hill known on the moor as Down Ridge. This we did not mount, but continued along its side, with the Wobrook below us on our right hand, until we reached the Holne road, which crosses this stream at Saddle Bridge. A new bridge is now built (in fact has been built for some years) close to the site of the old one, which was a very picturesque erection, being covered with ivy. The Wobrook in this part of its course marks the bounds between the forest and Holne Moor.

Turning in the direction of Hexworthy, a small moorland settlement about half a mile or so distant, we followed the road to it, where at the Forest Inn, a snug little hostelry, kept by my good old friend Richard Cleave, and which offers shelter and homely Dartmoor fare to the traveller, we made ourselves at home.

Here an incident occurred which caused me much amusement. We were sitting in the little parlour, not sorry to rest after our walk, when H——, in a fit of abstraction, took up a jug which stood near him, and began to play the "devil's tattoo" with it upon the table. Now, it is always the custom in our country public houses to knock upon the table with the jug, in order to summon the landlord, when it needs replenishing, and consequently Mrs. Cleave, the good landlady, hearing the sounds, imagined we were in want of something, and came to the door. I informed her, however, that we had not summoned her, and she withdrew, but the reason of her appearance was unknown to H—— who was entirely unaware of having been the cause of calling her in. Unfortunately my friend H—— is rather deaf, and being somewhat tired and not wishing to trouble him with any explanation, I let the matter drop. However, not more than a few minutes elapsed before H—— was repeating the "devil's tattoo," if anything with more gusto than before, and again Mrs. Cleave appeared. I explained to her that my friend being a Londoner was unacquainted with our system of knocking for attendance, and had merely been playing with the mug by drumming it on the table, and that we had not intended to call her. Mrs. Cleave did not seem quite satisfied with this explanation, evidently having a suspicion that we were playing her a trick, and the unconcerned expression which H——'s face wore, and which she took to be assumed, tended to increase this. When she withdrew H——, who had not heard a word of what had been said, turned to me with a puzzled look, exclaiming,

" What the dickens does the landlady want ? "

" Oh " I replied " its all right ; she only wants to know whether we require anything."

But a very few minutes elapsed, before H——, quite unconscious of what he was about, repeated his drumming on the table, in the midst of which he was interrupted by the landlady bursting into the room, with a bell, which she hastily put down on the table, exclaiming at the same time—

" There, if you want me you must ring ;   I shan't answer any more knocks ! "   And she left the room as quickly as she had entered it.

All this was quite incomprehensible to H——, who seemed to imagine that the landlady was very pressing in her endeavours to get us to order something more, and I scarcely knew which tickled me most,—his surprised look at the frequent appearance of Mrs. Cleave, or her evident idea that she was being " sold."

The Devonshire peasantry are very particular in the observance of certain customs, or recognized rules, when drinking together, and in this connection I am reminded of a superstition which Samuel Drew, in his *History of Cornwall*, mentions as existing in his time, and in which he considered he saw vestiges of a Druidical custom. It was deemed unlucky, he says, when a company of men were drinking together, to pass the glass around against the sun, or to describe a circle on any occasion, otherwise than by proceeding from the north to the east, and thence by the south and west to north again.

I know of no more interesting view in the whole of Dartmoor than is to be obtained from the door of the Forest Inn at Hexworthy. Grander and more romantic ones there certainly are, and it possesses, of course, none of the extreme wildness that is to be seen in the desolate portions of both the north and south quarters, nor can it be said, on account of the number of enclosures around, to form a truly representative picture of Dartmoor scenery, but for interest and beauty, and an exhibition of the mingling of wildness with the efforts of the cultivator, none can surpass it within the bounds of the moor. In the valley the West Dart is seen sweeping round a low hill, with Huccaby farm house surrounded by a few sycamore trees, near its bank. Above this the plantations of Brimpts are visible, and a rough piece of common, covered in summer with golden furze. Beyond, the granite crest of Yar Tor, presenting a truly noble outline, looks over the whole, while near it Dartmeet Hill, with the road winding up over its steep side, is in full view. Close to us the three or four farm houses that compose the settlement of Hexworthy are seen nestling in a hollow, with some sycamore trees spreading their branches around as if to shelter them, and two or three cottages may be observed at a short distance off upon the slope above.

Though there are but these few habitations, yet it is not very many years ago that the place boasted two public houses! At that time Gobbett Mine, which is close by, was being worked, and these houses of entertainment were opened for the special benefit of the miners—*and the landlords.*

While we had been resting the mist had gradually cleared away, and once more the sun burst brightly forth. Leaving the Forest Inn, under the roof of which I have spent many months at a time, my associations with the neighbourhood being some of the most pleasant of my recollections, we bent our steps through Hexworthy, and passing over the new-takes, descended to the Dart. The river was swollen by recent rains, and no place where we might cross by leaping from rock to rock presented itself. Higher up there are stepping stones, but these would have been covered, so high had the river risen, so not wishing to lose any time, we selected a spot and waded through the stream, the water reaching considerably above our knees. At a short distance above the confluence of the Swincombe river with the Dart (below which we crossed) there is now a wooden foot bridge or clam, thrown over the latter stream, but this did not exist at the time of which I am writing, having been only erected a few years.

Mounting the steep bank we crossed the road, and passing up by the ruined buildings which were connected with Brimpts Mine, we pointed straight for Loughter Tor.* On the slope of this tor, near the summit, is a kind of small cattle pound, an oblong enclosure with high walls, having a

---

* Or perhaps more correctly, Lough Tor. On the moor it is always called Laughter Tor.

gateway on its higher side. It is jocularly reputed to have been constructed as *"a measure for sheep"*! Instead of counting the animals they were driven within this enclosure, and as *the exact number of sheep it would contain was known*, when it was full all trouble of counting was unnecessary, and so it was said the sheep *instead of being numbered, were measured*!

From Loughter Tor we descended to the East Dart, and made our way towards Bellaford Bridge. At some distance down the river, on its left bank, is a small ruined building, known in the neighbourhood as Snails' House, in connection with which the following story has been told me on the moor.

Many years ago—probably at that indefinite period known as "once upon a time"—there dwelt at White Slade, as the house was then called,—two females, who would have been termed by the lawyers, spinsters, and in common parlance, old maids. They cultivated no garden, they possessed no flocks or herds, and how they lived was a mystery to the few neighbours who dwelt around. Their dwelling was in a very lonely spot, and for what reason they fixed upon it as their abode was equally a puzzle. All sorts of guesses were hazarded, but nothing authentic could be learned, as the inmates were very reserved, and but seldom held any communication at all with those around them. It was noticed, however, that they looked remarkably plump, and as such good bodily condition could only be maintained by an excellent and plentiful diet, where or how they obtained this perplexed the good gossips of the neighbourhood in no small degree.

At length it began to be hinted that they were in the habit of making free with the sheep pastured on the moor, and that good store of mutton found its way to White Slade. This rumour found favour with many, but there were others who shook their heads, and darkly hinted at something worse, saying that all the witches in the county had not been burned yet. A watch was set upon the house, but no signs of anything in the shape of food being conveyed to it were discovered, and yet the inmates, whenever they were seen, always presented the same buxom appearance. Curiosity was inflamed, and it was determined to bring matters to a conclusion by going in a body to the house, demanding admittance, and finding out from whence they obtained their supply of food. Accordingly a number of folks from the moor farms for some distance around met one day, and proceeded to White Slade with this end in view, and on approaching the house were readily admitted. They found the two women looking as fat and cheery as possible, but not a scrap of food could they see. They searched all over the house, but no bread nor meat was visible. At last in one part of the premises they discovered a row of several large pans, similar to what are used in the farm houses for putting butter in. Here, no doubt, was the food upon which the inmates subsisted; now they should see whether their suppositions about the sheep stealing were correct or not. Impatiently they dragged them forth to the light, and found they were full, not of choice cuts of mutton, but of *black slugs, preserved in salt !*

On this not very tempting, but seemingly exceedingly fattening food, the couple had subsisted, though whether from that time forth it lost its virtue or they lost their appetite is not known, but certain it is that the women's plump appearance soon became a thing of the past, and they gradually pined away until there were no more miserable looking beings upon the moor. And this is how the ruined dwelling near Loughter Hall came to be known as Snails' House.

Arriving at Bellaford Bridge—a modern county erection over the East Dart—I showed H—— the old clapper bridge which is situated immediately below it. This ancient structure consists of a buttress on each side of the river, and two piers, forming three openings for the water. Unfortunately the impost that spanned the centre opening is missing (as also are some more of its stones) so that the bridge is impassable. It is not to be seen in the bed of the stream, and for a long time I considered that the builders of the new bridge might perhaps have thrown it off, and used it in the construction of their erection. A few years ago, however, I discovered the perpetrator of this act of vandalism, a man who still lives on the moor, and who on my happening to refer to the old bridge in the course of conversation, informed me that he, when a boy, with a companion contrived to slide the stone off the piers.

This was done solely for mischief, and, as my informant explained, when he and his fellow delinquent ought to have been at school, which was held at the farm house near by. When they reached the house the pedagogue met them with black looks, " An' didn' he lace us," said my informant, " no fear 'bout that." My heart warmed towards the worthy school-master for showing in such a practical manner his detestation of the wantoness which had partially destroyed such an interesting old relic, and I intimated such to the narrator, when he immediately convinced me of my mistake in imagining that any feelings of this sort influenced that good man, by exclaiming,

"Oh, twudn' that; he laced us cos us was late to school!"

That an object so interesting should have been injured in this wilful manner is a matter of great regret. The stone seems to have disappeared, and what has become of it I am unable to say.

Since leaving Hexworthy the weather had been delightful, the sun shining out brightly, so that we were able to thoroughly enjoy the beautiful scenery encountered on our route. After halting awhile by the old bridge, listening to the music of the waters, we turned our faces up the stream, and by the left, or eastern, bank, made our way to Post Bridge, a moorland settlement about a mile distant. This is situated on the road running over Dartmoor from Plymouth to Exeter, lying midway between them, its distance from each being twenty miles.

On arriving here we entered the house of entertainment, now a temperance house, but at that time and for several years afterwards, being known as the Greyhound Inn, and while resting ourselves, talked upon matters pertaining to the neighbourhood with a moor-man whom we found there.

We could not, however, permit ourselves to stay long, as it was now getting late in the afternoon. We had by this time covered several miles since setting out, and as we had lingered to examine various interesting objects and bits of scenery by the way, many hours had been consumed, and I was anxious, before leaving, for H—— to inspect the ancient clapper bridge there, which is the finest example to be seen. This is similar to the one at Bellaford, consisting of three openings, but is altogether of larger proportions. At that time one of the huge slabs which had spanned the centre opening, lay in the bed of the stream, but has since been replaced upon the piers,—a very praiseworthy act, though unfortunately it has not been laid quite in its original position.*

I was out at Post Bridge about a month previously to my visit to it with H —--when I made some enquiries as to how this stone came to be thrown off the bridge, and gathered that it had been intentionally done. An old man whom I saw told me that he remembered when it was in its place on the piers, and said it had been thrown off about fifty years before. From what I have been able to learn, it appears that the slab was displaced with the intention of forming a sort of barrier with it in the bed of the stream across the centre opening, the operator hoping it would have fallen on its edge, and so by resting against the two piers have formed a wall, or dam, across that part of the stream, under which the water would have found its way. His design was also to place barriers across the other two openings, and so to form a kind of pond, where his ducks might disport themselves and be prevented from going down stream. The stone, however, fell on its face, and so rendered his plan abortive. I forbear to mention names but the person who is said to have done this still lives on the moor, and is now a very old man.

---

* I have given a description, with the measurements, of this old bridge, in the first volume of the *Western Antiquary*, (1881) and in another place in the same volume of that magazine have made mention of several others that exist on the moor.

Many of the most interesting of our Dartmoor Monuments have been entirely destroyed in this thoughtless manner, and it is a matter for congratulation that the fine old clapper at Post Bridge was not more seriously damaged. In the early part of the present century the old bridges of Dartmoor must have been in a complete state of preservation. The partial destruction of the one at Bellaford is even of later date than the removal of the stone from that we have just been referring to, the clapper at Dartmeet, as I have mentioned in Chapter I was swept away by a flood in the year 1826, and another which was thrown across the Blackabrook, to the north of the road between Rundle Stone and Two Bridges, and almost close to Fice's Well, was demolished by the rushing stream when swollen by rains, as late as 1873.

When such interesting objects are wilfully destroyed one cannot too strongly condemn the perpetrators of such acts of vandalism, but when overthrown by the operation of natural causes, though we deplore the unfortunate occurrence our feelings are, of course, in no way outraged. The Dartmoor Preservation Association, it is stated, are contemplating the restoration of these fallen bridges on the moor. While I will yield to none in my desire to see all our old monuments preserved, and am wishful to see their restoration effected, where such can *truly* be carried out, I cannot say that I view this proposal with feelings of any very great satisfaction. That I admire such an act as the replacing of the stone on the clapper at Post Bridge, it is un-necessary for me to say, because in such an instance we know that the restoration is proceeding on correct lines, and if the stones that have been taken away from the one at

Bellaford could be found and their positions determined, I should rejoice at seeing them placed once more upon the piers. But if an attempt be made to re-erect those which have been swept away by the floods, I am afraid that nothing which the antiquary will be able to point to with pride will be accomplished. Of what possible interest could the building of a clapper bridge at Dartmeet be to anybody now. The stones which composed the old bridge are nearly all swept into the river, and no one can tell what their original positions in the structure were. If it is " restored," the utmost that can be said will be that a new bridge has been built on the site, and from the materials, of an old one. Far better that those which have been spared to us, and which possess a real interest, should be well cared for, and by the exercise of suitable precautions guarded against the hand of the vandal and the encroachments of time, so that posterity may be able to thank us for handing down to them a real relic of antiquity, and not a sham.

Leaving Post Bridge we turned south-westward on the road to Princetown, which we followed for nearly two miles and a half when we turned aside, and passing up the slope of Crockern Tor, which is not very far from the road, gained the summit of that interesting spot. After H——had inspected it, and I had given him some slight account of the old Stannary Parliament which used to assemble on its exposed crest, we struck out for Wistman's Wood, as I was desirous H——should visit that exceedingly curious place, and the mile which lay between us and it was soon covered.

Wistman's Wood is sometimes incorrectly spoken of as being a remnant of a forest which once covered the whole, or the greatest part of the moor. That Dartmoor was never clothed in such manner is certain. There may, it is true, have been timber similar to the oaks of Wistman, growing in some of the more sheltered spots, in fact more than one such collection of trees are still to be seen there, and trunks of trees have been found imbedded in the peat,* which prove that such was the case, but that the moor ever possessed trees to any extent is an idea which cannot be entertained by anyone who is thoroughly acquainted with the district. Its designation of "forest" has been considered by some to be a proof of its having in former times been covered with trees, whereas such is really no proof at all of this having been so. The term "forest" by no means necessarily implies a district covered entirely with thick woods, but was given to those large tracts of land where the beasts of the chase were hunted, and which were under the forest laws, as formerly the whole of Devonshire was, until the reign of King John, when the county, with the exception of Dartmoor and Exmoor, was dis-afforested.

Wistman's Wood consists of a number of small oak trees growing in the midst of a clatter of rocks that stretches along the left bank of the West Dart, about a mile above Two Bridges. They are not of great height, averaging about ten or twelve feet, but are of very aged appearance. It is said that a Perambulation of the forest made in the time of the Conqueror, describes the old wood as presenting much the same appearance as it does to-day. There is no such a thing as walking through it,—the passage of the wood must be made entirely by scrambling from rock to rock, and great care is necessary, for these are so overgrown with moss, that a false step would quickly

---

* I have myself seen such dug out.

precipitate the explorer into one of the crevices that everywhere abound. From amid these boulders the gnarled trunks of the trees protrude, their lower limbs not infrequently resting on the surfaces of them. Trunks and limbs are all covered with a thick coating of moss, which causes them to appear much larger than they really are. The whole is of a very interesting character, which is heightened by its wild surroundings.

In the summer of 1886, by some means, never definitely ascertained, this old wood after surviving the hundreds of winter storms that have swept over it, took fire, and was very seriously injured. I shall never forget my feelings of sorrow when I visited it about six weeks after this calamity happened. The upper portion of the wood was nothing but a mass of charred and blackened boughs, that rose up out of the rocks like dark spectres bewailing the loss of their former sylvan beauty. Here and there a tree, which by some miraculous good fortune had escaped the flames, still flourished its green arms around, but only to make the extent of the ravages of the fire among its less happy companions yet more clearly to be realized. I had heard of this sad circumstance just after its occurrence, but I was not prepared to see so much havoc made in the old wood. As I looked upon the scene I could scarcely believe that this was the ancient grove of oaks that I had known so long, and I felt genuine sorrow that an old friend should have been overtaken by so unfortunate a fate.

It is considered that the wood took fire through the heating of dead leaves, and was not caused, as was at first supposed, by carelessness or incendiarism. I offer no opinion as to this. Two gentlemen had visited the wood just before the fire was discovered, and it was thought possible that they may have dropped a lighted match, and un-intentionally set fire to the dead leaves but they both affirmed that such was not the case. Mr. Charles Barrington —the bailiff of Dartmoor—happened to see the smoke rising from the wood, from near Tor Royal, his residence, and without loss of time mounted his horse and rode away to it, but it was found to be impossible to check the progress of the flames. Hopes, however, are entertained that the trees though utterly disfigured for the time, have not all been killed, but that most of them will again put forth their shoots, and flourish as of old.

But my visit to the old wood with H—— was twelve years before this calamity, and we saw it in all its summer beauty. After spending some time beneath its gnarled and twisted boughs, we passed down to the river which flows along its foot, and as the sun was declining made our way down the valley to Two Bridges.

On reaching this spot we were surprised at observing a knot of men, engaged in some sports, on the river's bank, not far from the inn, but of which I soon found the cause. It was the day after Two Bridges Fair, which was generally devoted to amusement, and a wrestling match was going forward. Here was an opportunity for H—— to see some true Devonshire sport, and we accordingly looked on for a short time at the bout which was being played. In the " stickler," or referee, I noticed a Plymouth man well-known in that capacity, and the contest over which he was presiding seemed to possess great interest for the lookers-on, who were evidently thoroughly enjoying themselves.

Turning from this sight, as the evening was getting

advanced, we mounted the hill in front of us, and following the road to Princetown, were very soon snugly ensconced within the walls of the Duchy. Here another incident in which my friend H—— unconsciously caused me some amusement occurred. A party from Plymouth, who had been spending the day at Princetown, were just about to take their departure in a wagonette. We were alone in the bar, and H—— had thrown himself into Mr. Rowe's—the proprietor's—arm chair, being naturally very tired with our long day's walk. It was getting nearly dark and the bar was not yet lighted, when one of the excursionists with his rug over his arm, opened the door, and seeing H—— in the armchair mistook him for the host, and wished him farewell, expressing at the same time the pleasure the day at Princetown had afforded him. H—— looked enquiringly at me, without, however, gaining any explanation of the circumstance, for I was quite content to let matters take their course, and play the part of spectator. Turning again to the visitor, and gathering from his gestures that he was bidding him farewell, he wished him good night in a pleasant manner, and the former withdrew, evidently imagining that he had been taking leave of the landlord, while H——, not grasping the situation at all, seemed to be rather at a loss to account for the eccentricities of people on Dartmoor.

We rested ourselves for some time at the Duchy, and then once more resumed our journey, setting out for Siward's Cross by the same route which I have indicated, in the previous chapter, as taking when on my ramble with my man, George.

Siward's Cross, like Melrose Abbey, may well be visited

by the pale moonlight. That this old memorial of other times fails not to impress the beholder even more than when seen at noon-day, I can vouch for, having stood beside it when I have been able to exclaim with Colma, " Lo! the calm moon comes forth. The flood is bright in the vale. The rocks are grey on the steep." * But on this particular night no expectations filled us of seeing it bathed in the moonbeams, for such were not, and when we reached the venerable old monument it was pitch dark.

Not many weeks before I had passed it in the bright sunshine of a summer's morning, when everything around was speaking of life and happiness, when the lark carolled in the sky, and the cattle browsing on the slopes seemed to show that they were enjoying the influence of the glorious orb of day. Now, all was dark upon the heath; the sky was of an inky black, and objects but a very few yards distant quite undiscernable. I was therefore merely able to show H—— the old cross, but it was too dark for him to examine it at all; and I doubt whether he would have felt much inclined to have done so even if there had been light sufficient for such a purpose, for the fatigues of the journey were beginning to tell upon him (and on myself, too, for that matter) and his thoughts were only of rest.

Proceeding up the hill to the southward, very slowly and wearily it must be confessed, we at length reached the summit, and sat down to rest ourselves. Our short sojourn at Princetown had not been of much value to us; it was only temporary relief, and in fact had made us feel more tired than we were before, as the cessation from walking had

---

* Ossian. The Songs of Selma.

caused us to get stiff, and on re-commencing the exercise
felt irksome.   My friend H——— now began to grow sleepy,
and I had as much as I could do to prevent him dozing off.
I daresay he thought it rather unkind of me, when I rudely
shook him, and bade him keep awake, but while I was quite
content to sit and rest, and amuse myself with looking at
the few stars which were beginning to shine forth, I knew
it would never do to fall asleep on the moor, for though it
was summer time the night air on this elevated spot was
extremely chilly.

As I sat contemplating H——— who lay on the ground near
me, I pondered in my mind what it was best to do. If we
pushed onward across the moor we should have a long
trudge over rough ground, which owing to the intense
darkness would, in H———'s sleepy condition, be a very
uncomfortable journey, and we should be unable to reach
home until daybreak, for a good many miles lay between
us and Brent, and our tired condition rendered it impossible
for us to make very great speed.   I did not, however, wish
to retrace my steps by going back to Princetown, so after
turning it over in my mind, I came to the conclusion that I
would shape my course for Dousland Barn, where we could
knock the inmates up, and get a few hours' rest, proceeding
on our journey in the early morning.

When I unfolded this scheme to H———,explaining to him
that Dousland Barn was an inn, it commended itself to him
as a most sensible one, and I believe the visions of a
comfortable chamber, with good, clean sheets, which I
judged were passing in mental array before him, proved a
great incentive to the shaking off of his drowsiness.   We
accordingly arose, and turned our faces in the direction I

had determined upon pursuing, but we had to walk with
great caution, for it was as dark as a dungeon. There was
no fear of our hurrying very much, our fatigued and jaded
state precluded that, but proceeding even at an ordinary
pace was not to be attempted without care, and frequently
had we to feel the ground in front of us with our sticks, the
blackness of the night preventing us from seeing a step of
the way. However, this was no inconvenience to us beyond
causing us to be rather longer over our walk than we wished,
for I knew by the nature of the ground we were traversing,
that we were holding the right course Making in the
direction of Down Tor, I descended to a branch of the Mew,
and crossing near a farm called Kingsett, gained a moor
road not very far from Lether Tor Bridge, and proceeded
along this to Lowery, a farm just on the borders of the
moor. From here a walk by the road of about a mile
brought us to Dousland Barn, which my friend H——— was
not at all sorry for.

The night was now far advanced, and as it would not be
long ere daylight broke I began to consider that it was
scarcely worth while to arouse the inmates, and suggested
that we should make ourselves comfortable in the porch of
the inn until daybreak, when if we found we had taken
sufficent rest to enable us to go forward in comfort, we
should set out for home, following the road leading by
Meavy over the moor to Cornwood. I thought this would
be a better plan than going to bed, for I knew that we
should feel very unwilling to leave our pillows early, so tired
were we, and wishing to be back to Brent in the forenoon
I was not willing that we should stay about very long. I
therefore came to the conclusion that it would be wiser to

take a temporary rest, under shelter, for a few hours,
and then in the early morning, with daylight to cheer us,
accomplish the remaining portion of our journey.

Accordingly we ensconced ourselves in a corner of the
porch, which like many of the old fashioned structures of
the kind was fitted with benches,* and gave ourselves such
a rest as was by no means to be despised, and in this
manner waited the coming of the dawn. This appeared
at last, and while it was yet scarce light enough to
see, we took our way along the side of Yennadon to
Merchant's Bridge near Meavy, and then ascended Lynch
Hill. As we crossed the down we saw the sun just
peeping over the hills on our left,—the second sunrise
we had witnessed during our walk,—and as we felt the
warming rays our spirits began to revive, and we enjoyed
fully the delightful influence of the soft and balmy morning
air. At Cadaford Bridge we paused awhile to observe the
beautiful scene around us, and leaning on the parapet looked
down upon the merry laughing waters of the rolling Plym,
which sparkling in the bright beams of the early morning
sun, hastened onwards like a thing of life, as if happy in the
birth of a new day.

Up the hill we took our way, with the tors of Trowlsworthy on our left, and on approaching the top of the
ascent came in view of Roman's Cross, which stands by the
roadside, fixed firmly in a socket stone of granite. From
this point a beautiful prospect opened to our view, which in
the soft air of the morning was rendered yet more charming.

---

* A new hotel has only recently been built, close to the old building,
and another at a few hundred yards distant, on the opposite side of the
road. This is one result of the Princetown Railway.

The moor lay all around us, calm and quiet, but being, as we were, so close to its borders, a view of a very different nature was seen beyond it, the contrast serving to enhance the beauties belonging to the both. Here, the quiet heath, with the music of the lark;—there, green fields and wooded slopes with homesteads and hamlets dotted about, and away by the bay yonder the good old town of Plymouth, not yet aroused from the slumber of the night. The prospect was one exceeding interest, its contemplation as we pursued our way, enabling us for a time to forget our fatigues.

Passing the Lee Moor Clay Works, and crossing the Torry, we soon after descended the hill and left the moor at its foot. And here commenced the most trying part of the journey to H——. Our tramp had been a long one, with no sleep for two nights. This was telling upon us now, but more particularly upon my friend, who was not accustomed to such journies as I had been in the habit of making, and the oft-repeated question of "How much farther is it?" showed me that he had had very nearly enough of walking. However, we reached Cornwood at last, and only a mile lay between us and the station. This we soon covered, and after waiting a short time took the early morning train for Brent, where we arrived at about half past seven.

H—— limped sadly away, and I saw him no more till the following day. He reached his house, at once went to bed, and did not rise till the next morning. When I met him again he was wearing a pair of canvas shoes, finding it impossible to get on his boots, for not having been provided with the stout laced boots necessary for such a tramp, he had worn a pair of ordinary ones with elastic sides, and in pulling them off, it seems, he had quite stripped the skin from his heels, and the canvas shoes were the only things he could wear on his feet during the remainder of his visit to Brent.   As for myself, on reaching home I first took a cold bath, then ate a hearty breakfast, and went about the ordinary duties of the day, resting a little in the afternoon but not retiring until my usual hour.

If the reader will trace our route on a map of Dartmoor, he will see that we covered a good deal of ground, and adding to this the numerous detours we made to examine objects by the way, it is scarcely any wonder that my friend H—— found himself so thoroughly used up at the end of our ramble.

CHAPTER V.

THE ERME VALLEY, AND RAMBLE TO GREAT MISTOR.

RISING with the lark one beautiful morning in the summer of the year following that of my ramble with H——, I left home with two companions and my retriever Nero, for a day's jaunt over the moor. My intention was to visit one or two objects on the border of the south quarter of the forest, and also to push on through Princetown to Holming Beam and Great Mistor. We proceeded first to Shipley Bridge and on to Petre's Cross by the same route as I have indicated in Chapter III, but instead of following the old tram-road to its end, when we reached the place where the Abbots' Way crosses it, we left it and made our way by the latter path to Red Lake Ford. Red Lake is a small stream rising in some mires near here, and, as its name indicates, is of a very red colour. After a short course it falls into the Erme, the point of confluence forming one of the forest boundaries, the line, according to the perambulations, running from Western Whitaburrow to the spot in question.

As we crossed the slope of Green Hill, the Erme valley was in full view, with the silvery stream meandering through it, its bosom reflecting the bright beams of the early morning sun. This valley, so quiet and deserted now, was in days gone by the scene of man's busy labours. The remains of ancient settlements are numerous, and the evidences of the former operations of the tin streamer exist from its source almost down to Harford Bridge, the place where the river leaves the moor. Close to the spot where it rises are some deep excavations known as Erme Pits, which are very curious. They are of some considerable extent, and a vast amount of labour must have been performed by the tinners at this spot in their search for metal.

Not far below its source the Erme receives a stream known as Dark Lake, much larger than itself, and which flows down from the boggy ground that constitutes the most elevated portion of the south quarter of the forest. This stream well deserves its name, for the rocks in its channel are almost entirely covered with black moss. One of the paths to which I have alluded in Chapter III, and which are known to very few besides moor-men, leads from the head of Dark Lake to the gulf to the southward of Fox Tor, thus forming a fine pass through the bogs, from the valley of the Erme to that of the Swincombe river. On the moor it is called Black Lane, and is of the greatest use to the moor-men of this part of Dartmoor. As before observed, it is a knowledge of these paths which enables one to make his way over the moor with safety and comfort. I have passed through Black Lane at all seasons,—sometimes the surrounding ground being such that locomotion on foot would have been almost impossible, (on horseback the bogs adjoining can never be crossed) yet this path was good and firm, and is always so, even at the very worst time of the winter

Not a great way below the head of Dark Lake is a very extensive stream work, and near it is one of the many little nooks on the moor to which I have fancifully given names, and set apart as my resting-places. Below this it runs between steep and rocky banks into the Erme, joining that stream on its left bank, and at no very great distance below this, another tributary joins the Erme on the same side, flowing from a spot the moor-men call Middle Mires, and yet further on Red Lake runs into it. On the opposite side two little streams augment the waters of the main river, so that within a distance of about a mile from its source, the Erme receives no less than five streams. On the banks of each of these are the remains of the works of the tin miner, as also is the case with the tributaries which it receives lower down its course.

At the point where Red Lake helps to swell its waters the Erme makes a bend, and at a little over a quarter of a mile below this, on its eastern bank, is Erme Pound, an enclosure of great interest. It was formerly used for the purpose of penning cattle in, found, pastured on the moor by those who had not the right so to do, at the time of the forest drifts. At certain periods of the year these drifts, as they are termed, take place, the moor being then driven or searched for cattle, and such as are found on it without their owners being known to the moor-men are impounded. At the present time Dunnabridge Pound, on the West Dart, is the place where estrays are kept, but formerly there were other pounds in addition to that, and Erme Pound was one of these. It is mentioned in old records, and was, no doubt, the pound to which all estrays found in the south quarter were driven.

G

A careful examination made of it many years ago, led me to believe that it is constructed on the site of a more ancient enclosure—that of a hut settlement, and constant visits to it from that day to this have tended to confirm me in this opinion. There can be no doubt that the wall is raised upon what once formed the foundations of a rude vallum, such as is now seen encircling many of the ancient enclosures on the moor,—two of which, by the way, in a state of splendid preservation, are situated very near to the pound. A similar arrangement of raising a wall on the lines of a more primitive enclosure may also be seen at Dunnabridge Pound,—as is pointed out by Mr. Bray,—for I am convinced that he is perfectly correct in his opinion as to such being the case. Within Erme Pound are the vestiges of hut circles, while a great portion of its area is covered with large stones, as also is the ground immediately without it on its western and southern sides, the pound being situated, so to speak, at one end of a clatter of rocks. Immediately without the wall, on its northern side, the ground is quite clear, scarcely a single stone encumbering it, and it therefore seems difficult to understand why such a desirable spot for an enclosure for penning cattle in should have been rejected in favour of one thickly strewn with granite blocks, had not some strong inducement to select the latter presented itself. Such inducement the constructors found in the materials which had formed the vallum of the ancient enclosure, and which enabled them to build their wall without being at the trouble of bringing stones to its site.

Why such a rocky spot should have originally been chosen for an enclosure at all is not very clear, but we can more readily understand its being done where the object was merely to pen cattle at night, than we can conceive its being fixed upon for a pound where cattle would have to be confined for several days together. It is only the lower portion of the enclosure that could afford pasturage, it being there, for a small space, free from rocks.

The pound is of an irregular shape, though somewhat approaching a circular form, and the measurements I have taken of it show it to be three hundred and forty-five yards in circumference. It is situated at the foot of the hill known as Brown Heath, the Erme flowing within a few yards of its wall.

The entrance to the pound is on its southern side, and consists of a wide gateway. Immediately outside this gateway are the remains of a very curious building, and lower down, but close to the wall of the pound, the ruins of another of similar size, but of different internal arrangement. In shape they resemble the oblong buildings which I have mentioned as being frequently found on or near the site of old mining operations on the moor, and the situation of those in question, quite near to such workings, would seem to show that it was for purposes connected with such that they were erected. This, however, we cannot be sure of, for it is by no means improbable that they were constructed as places of shelter for those who visited the pound at the time of the drifts, for there are no habitations within several miles of it.

The hut which so closely adjoins the gateway has a stone bench running almost entirely around the interior, forming a seat capable of accommodating a number of persons, and at such a time, when many would be gathered at the drift, would certainly have proved a most useful shelter. This building, which runs east and west, is twenty-two feet long and twelve feet wide, and the walls are about four feet in height. The entrance is in the corner, at the eastern end of the northern side, facing the wall of the pound. The stone benches are about fifteen inches high, and twenty-two inches wide, and when roofed over this little hut must have proved a convenient refuge during inclement weather. I have frequently made it a resting-place, and remember on one occasion being there with a friend, (who not long after left our shores for a distant land, in order to spread the knowledge of the gospel,) when we were overtaken by a sudden shower, from which we sheltered ourselves by crouching down on the bench in one corner of the little building, and opening that very useful article,—but one which I certainly never carry on the moor,—*an umbrella.* My friend, however had come provided with one, and, though forming no part of the impediment of a Dartmoor trotter, it at all events shielded us that day from a Dartmoor shower.

The seat or bench within this building, runs, as I have said, almost entirely around its interior, and I have been informed that a similar arrangement prevails at the present day, at the Cornish mines, in the houses used by the miners for the purpose of changing their clothes, before and after going underground. This, if so, is evidence in favour of the mining character of the hut, but why, when such buildings are dotted all over the moor, this one near the pound happens to be the only one in which such an arrangement of seats occurs, is difficult, when regarding it in such a light, to understand. And it is equally difficult to see what reason there could be for choosing such an awkward place for the erection of mining huts. Both this and the one near to it, are built in the midst of a clatter of rocks, and are not approachable with any degree of comfort—a state of things which is more easily understood if we regard them as being merely for temporary use at the time of the forest drifts.

The second house is of similar size, but the walls are rather higher, one gable end being almost intact. This one does not possess any seats. The entrance is in the corner, and seems to have been sheltered by a kind of porch, the remains of a low wall being still to be seen, which sprang from the main wall by the side of the doorway, and then turned, at the distance of a few feet, so as to run parallel with it for a little distance, thus forming a short passage by its side,—a plan which I have seen adopted in many of the huts on the moor. This building has the appearance of having been a habitation, probably used temporarily, if it was connected with the pound. Of course, these two little buildings may have been erected originally as mining huts, and adapted afterwards to the purposes of the moor-men at the drifts. In a dilapidated enclosure close by there are one or two others which are undoubtedly miners' buildings.

Near Erme Pound there is a most interesting collection of pre-historic remains, and I have spent many and many a day in their examination. Below the pound the river after passing between rather steep banks flows into an open space covered with the remains of the tin streamer. On each side of this a combe runs up into the higher ground, the largest being that on its left bank, which is known as Stoney Bottom, and down which flows a little stream by the name of Hook Lake, in which we probably see the Celtic term *ock*, signifying *water*, and which appears in the name of the two

Ockments, in the north quarter of the moor. Around here I
have found several of the little mining buildings of the usual
type, and there is one which I once chanced upon which is of
more than usual interest, and which is evidently an old
blowing house, similar to the one on the Avon below Heng
Lake, and which I have described in Chapter III. It is
situated immediately at the foot of Stoney Bottom, and in
making an examination of it several years since, I discovered
in it a large stone having cavities, somewhat similar to the
one lying outside the building just referred to, forming
moulds for the smelted tin. The building is reared against
a bank, in the manner so frequently adopted by the constructors of these huts, and measures externally, twenty-
seven feet in length, and seventeen feet and a half in width.
About one third of it is partitioned off by a wall, and in this
smaller compartment, a water wheel not improbably worked,
for I have been able to trace the remains of a water-course
from the Erme to this old building. The doorway is in a
similar position to that seen in most of the oblong mining
erections on the moor, that is to say, in the front, at a short
distance from the corner. It faces about south, and but a
few paces from it Hook Lake flows by, falling into the Erme
not many yards below.

The stone in which the moulds are cut lies not far within
the entrance, and is a large block of granite, five feet long
by two feet wide. On its surface is one complete mould and
one broken one. That still uninjured measures exactly one
foot in length, and about three and a half inches wide, by
about three inches deep. It is rather narrower at the bottom
than at the top, so as to admit of the block of tin being taken
out easily. The broken mould, which is on the edge of the

stone, is of nearly the same length, but its width cannot be determined, one side being broken entirely away. The building is altogether a very interesting specimen of an old blowing-house, and the other remains of mining by which it is surrounded, are curious, and well worthy of inspection by the explorer of the moor.

The village enclosures near Erme Pound are fine examples of these ancient objects, the walls being constructed of very large blocks, and the hut circles, within and without them, being in a remarkably fine state of preservation. There is also an irregular enclosure, between these and the pound, in which the walls are of a totally different character—not nearly so cyclopean in their style,—and in this we may perhaps see an enclosure of the beginning of the sixteenth century, for in an account rendered by the forester of the south quarter, bearing date 1502-3, mention is made of the new rent of 1½d " of Thomas Rawe, John Beare and others for one acre of land on the common of Devon, lying neare to Yerme between Erme Pound and Quyocke Bemefote,* to hold to them according to the custom of the forest of Dartmore."

About a mile below Erme Pound, on the opposite bank of the river, is a very fine stone circle, fifty-four feet in diameter, only three of the stones, of the twenty-six of which it consists, having fallen.† A row of stones, singularly

---

* Quickbeam Foot. Quickbeam Hill, now generally called Erme Plains, lies to the southward of Stoney Bottom, and on the opposite side of it to Erme Pound.

† I mentioned this circle among other interesting objects on Dartmoor, in a communication to the second volume of the *Antiquary,* 1880.

perfect near the circle, extends from it for a considerable distance over the moor, terminating in a dilapidated kistvaen on the summit of Green Hill. The ground around this circle is remarkably free from rocks and stones, and it therefore stands out very prominently on the dark brown heath.

Further down the river, along which the *debris* of the streamer is heaped for some distance, and just opposite to a little feeder, known as Dry Lake, is a small rocky hollow, which forms a most charming retreat on a hot summer's day. The tourist following the course of the stream might pass it unobserved, hid away, as it is, in the side of the hill. It is an artificial excavation—the work of the miner—and one of a rare kind on the moor, as the ore has been extracted from amid hard granite rocks, where the "pocket" lay. Several trees, principally the quickbeam, or mountain ash, grow upon its edges and from its sides, springing from clefts in the rock, and also at its entrance, which they partially conceal. These throw a most grateful shade over the bottom of the hollow, and with various creeping plants overhanging its edges, render it a most pleasing spot, and from its contrast to the bare moor all around it, this almost fairylike grotto, will be doubly appreciated by the rambler who seeks it as a place of temporary rest when wandering through this valley.

Below this spot, and by the side of a small stream which falls into the Erme, is a little covered erection of the kind frequently seen on the moor, though not often in so complete a state as this, and which it is very likely were used by the miners as repositories for their tools. Mr. Spence Bate, in a paper on the *Pre-historic Antiquities of Dartmoor* in the fourth volume of the *Transactions of the Devonshire Association*, has described this curious little building.

THE ERME, ABOVE HARFORD BRIDGE.

Further down the river, a steep hill rises from its right bank, on the summit of which is a cairn known as Stalldon Barrow, and on the slope on the opposite side of the stream is Piles Wood, an ancient oak wood of a similar character to Wistman's Wood, only that the trees are not quite so large. It is a most charming spot, and one which it is difficult to surpass on Dartmoor. Below the wood the river courses on by extensive new-takes to Harford Bridge, where it leaves the moor.

It then flows through a most lovely valley to Ivybridge, and from thence, mid fine scenery, passes on by the village of Ermington and the grounds of Flete, and empties itself into the sea at Mothycombe.

I know of no stream on Dartmoor more interesting than the Erme. On its banks are to be seen examples of nearly every kind of pre-historic monument that is found on the moor, some of the finest village settlements, an interesting old drift pound, an ancient wood, numerous specimens of old mining houses, and the remains of extensive stream works. Upwards of a dozen tributaries flow into it, having their banks, like that of the main stream, covered with the vestiges of the operations of the tin seeker; in its channel are several small islands, formed by the stream here and there dividing into two branches and re-uniting a score or so of yards lower down, producing an interesting effect when viewed from the steep banks above. The scenery, too, all along its course, is thoroughly characteristic of Dartmoor, and many points of vantage its banks offer from which to obtain a variety of wild scenes. Beneath Stalldon Barrow, about midway up the slope, a good view, looking up stream, of the folding banks is obtained, and below, a fine picture of the river hurrying down the narrow pass formed on one side by the steep scarp of the hill and on the other by the precipitous descent under Sharp Tor and Three Barrows. Further down stream, flinging their green boughs around, and flourishing in the wilderness, stand the ancient oaks of Piles Wood, o'er-hanging the silvery river, and affording a sweet retreat to the feathered melodists which enliven the sombre old moor with their gladsome songs.

But we must onward, gentle reader, for the journey we have to perform is not a short one; no longer must we loiter on the slope of Greenhill looking down the valley of the Erme, but hasten across the forest that lies before us.

The stream flowing from Middle Mires was crossed, also Dark Lake, and the boggy ground of Crane Hill reached. Making our way with caution over this elevated ridge, where the cotton rush grows in the wet soil, frequently causing the ground, when viewed from a short distance, to look as though it were covered with flakes of snow, we soon commenced our descent to the upper waters of the Plym. Here, also, are extensive stream works, some of the operations in which were continued down to a very recent date. The whole hill, of which Eylesbarrow forms the summit, has been worked in every direction.* Towards the valley to the north-west, down which flows a branch of the Mew, and where again are further

---

* Mr. Burt in his Preface to Carrington's poem of Dartmoor (1826) states that Eylesbarrow Mine was then at work, and possessed a smelting house (the ruins of which may be seen) where one hundred blocks of tin were coined for Michælmas quarter. 1824. Of the correct spelling of this name I am not certain, sometimes it is rendered as I have here given it; in the Perambulations it is spelt Elysburghe and Elisboroughe. Mr. Burt gives Ailsborough, and this is generally heard upon the moor, though not un-frequently it is pronounced as if spelt Yelsborough.

workings of a most extensive character, these vestiges of mining are to be seen; they may also be observed extending towards Fox Tor Mire ; down the hill to the Plym, near Ditsworthy Warren; and to the valley of the Deancombe brook, where, near Combe Tor, are many deep excavations.

Passing over the ridge of Eylesbarrow, we shortly reached Siward's Cross, from whence a pleasant walk of about two and a half miles brought us to Princetown.

Here a rather amusing incident occurred. One of my companions had gone into a shop to purchase some bread for Nero, and with the other I was strolling on towards the prisons, when a woman ran out of a house that we had passed a minute or two previously, calling out at the top of her voice, and gesticulating wildly for us to stop. My companion ran back towards her, and while I followed more leisurely, I heard her shout out "Be you Mister Paddon's travellers ?" Mr. Paddon is a draper of Okehampton, and supplies goods to the villages on the moor. Our knapsacks were responsible for this mistake, the would-be purchaser of Mr. Paddon's wares, who was, I expect, a new arrival at Princetown, having mistaken us for packmen, and our knapsacks for what Tom Hood calls "the little back shop that such tradesmen carry."

Passing the gate of the prisons, we turned down the road that runs around them immediately without the wall, (and which has since been closed to the public) and went as far as the cemetery, where the French and American prisoners who died whilst at Princetown, were buried, and which is situated at the rear of the prisons. Here we could look up at the first of the new model prisons which have been built within the walls, and which had then not long been completed.

In this part of the establishment I have understood that the Tichborne Claimant was confined during his incarceration here

From near this point a path led across the prison enclosures to the road between Rundle Stone and the bridge over the Blackabrook. This we pursued, and gaining the road crossed it and made our way to the stream, which we also crossed, and thence proceeded to the site of some old mining operations on Holming Beam, a tract of moor which lays between the Blackabrook and the Cowsic. After an examination of these, and wandering for some distance over Holming Beam, we turned back to Great Mis Tor, upon reaching which we selected a sheltered spot, and proceeded to bivouac.

Great Mis Tor has been supposed by some to have derived its name from the heathen deity Misor, to whom they consider it probable its rocks were dedicated as an altar. For those who find amusement in giving the rein to their fancy to such an extent as to seriously believe they see in the granite tors of the moor temples of Druidism, such far-fetched derivations are easy to accept. They remind me of the instances given in Dean Swifts' satire, *Etymology in Earnest ; or Greek and Latin derived from English*, one of which occurs to me at the moment, which shows how the name of Alexander the Great originated from the words *"All eggs under the grate !"*—being a command given to a family who were dining off those comestibles, lest the fact should be discovered by some visitors who were observed drawing near the house ! It is probable that the tor in question owes its name to the mists which so frequently shroud the crests of our granite heights, its situation on the western edge of the moor, and its elevation, being such as to render it likely to be enveloped in these more often than some of its fellow tors.

The view from the summit of Great Mis Tor is truly grand, and no description can hope to do justice to it. On one side a fine view of the wild moor, and on the other an immense expanse of country,--hill and dale, river and sea,----with the Cornish range forming a far-off background. Yonder, like a thread of silver, is seen the Tamar, and the Royal Albert Bridge at Saltash is distinctly visible, and even as we gazed we saw the steam from a train as it approached Brunel's magnificent erection. On one of the huge piles that compose the tor is a curious cavity of the kind known as rock-basins, and which occur on many of the Dartmoor tors, though this on Mis Tor is much more regular in its formation than the generality of them. They are supposed by some to be artificial excavations, and to have been hollowed out for the purpose of containing rain water to be used in connection with Druidical rites, but most geologists now believe them to be due to the influence of natural causes. The one on Mis Tor is very curious, and well worth inspection, while the tourist who shall have climbed to the summit to examine it will be more than repaid for any trouble he may have taken in making the ascent, by the unsurpassable prospect which will meet his eye, and which we now stayed long upon the tor to enjoy. My companions—both Brent men—had never been so far upon the moor before, so the view was all new to them. The principal objects I pointed out to them, *after we had finished our meal*, for attractive though the view was, the cravings of appetite would not be set aside for anything. Nero, too, seemed glad to join us, and with his appetite, like ours, sharpened by the air and the long walk, soon made his loaf disappear.

After clambering among the piles of rock of this fine old tor, we descended towards Rundle Stone, and on reaching the bottom of the slope turned to gaze once more upon the granite crest we had just left. From whatever point Great Mis Tor is viewed it presents a grand and imposing appearance, and from many a spot in the wild old forest it may be seen lifting its crown of rocks above the dark ridges of the desolate parts of the moor.

The evening was now drawing to a close, so we walked briskly into Princetown, and after a short halt there, set out upon our homeward journey. At Siward's Cross we once more opened our wallets, and made a good supper, and then set out forward through the darkness for home. There was no mist of any kind, but so intensely dark was it, that it was impossible for us to see Nero, with his black coat, even when he was quite close to us, and lest he should stray away without our perceiving it, we tied a white handkerchief around his neck, in order that we might be able to keep an eye upon him. In this way we walked on, and I made a bee line for Shipley Bridge, which we reached thoroughly tired out with our long ramble.

We had now only about two miles more to walk, and this we quickly got over. We halted by the spring in Didworthy court, to take a draught of the sparkling water, and consulting my watch, I found the time was close upon two o'clock. The stars had just commenced to shine out a little, and with these tiny lamps twinkling here and there in the black sky, and seeming to cheer us by relieving, even if in so faint a manner, the darkness which had hung over us during our walk across the forest, we reached home and rest.

CHAPTER VI.

A DARTMOOR THUNDER-STORM.

ONE beautiful morning in the summer of the year 1878, when I was staying for several months on the moor at Hexworthy, I set out accompanied by my wife, taking with us our pet dog Snap—a thorough little Dartmoor ranger,—for a ramble over some of the high ground between the upper waters of the East and West Dart.

We proceeded by the road past Dunnabridge Pound, meeting the postman on our way, who gave us our letters, and then struck across the common towards Smith Hill, a small farm house on the banks of the Cherrybrook, and not far above the bridge which spans that stream near the enclosures of Prince Hall. The Cherrybrook is a tributary of the West Dart, the point of confluence being at no great distance below Prince Hall bridge. Passing Smith Hill we went across the new-take in the direction of the powder mills, and just before reaching the Princetown and Moreton road, we heard the low rumbling of thunder. Presently the sky became overcast, great black clouds covering the face of the heavens, and entirely shutting out the sunshine, while heavy drops of rain warned us that it would be well to seek shelter from the coming shower. Before, however, we could gain the building which lays near the road at the entrance to the powder mills the shower descended, the distant thunder still rumbling across the sky. Seeking the shelter of the new-take wall we crouched down while the shower continued, "waiting till the clouds rolled by," which fortunately did not tax our patience, for shortly, as if by magic, struggling beams of sunlight burst forth, and soon all was bright and golden as before.

This, however, did not continue long, for hardly had we gained the road, when again the gathering clouds warned us that we were to expect a repetition of the downpour, and the low muttering of the thunder once more was heard. Hastily making our way to the building just referred to, we took shelter under its roof, and not a moment too soon, for barely had we reached it than the rain again descended in torrents, and continued for some time.

I now began to think we should have to give up our contemplated ramble and return to Hexworthy, but after a time the sky once more cleared, and the rain ceasing the bright sun shone forth in all its glory, giving us hope of a fine day. Leaving our place of shelter we betook ourselves across the common behind Cherrybrook Farm, and ascended the hill, with Crockern Tor on our left hand. There was now no signs of further showers, everything looking bright and clear, and reaching the summit of the hill, and pausing awhile to admire the beautiful moorland prospect around us, we made our way along the ridge to Longaford Tor.

This tor, which is a very prominent object for a great distance around, is situated on the hill to the eastward of Wistman's Wood, and is of a conical form, presenting a very striking appearance, from whichever side it is viewed.

We clambered up its precipitous sides, and on the summit,
where there is a tiny plateau of fine grass, we spread our
luncheon, and while discussing it, also feasted our eyes
upon the attractive expanse of moor which that elevated
spot commands. Many and many a tor is to be seen from
Longaford, and immense stretches of wild heath and fen on
every side. Miss Sophie Dixon in her work *Castalian Hours*
has some charming verses on this tor, which are most
appropriate to our musings on that hoary pile of granite
rocks.

" Here, seated on thy rock-built tower,
  —A place of ancient days remote—
Our heart hath felt thy mountain power
  Our eyes thy mountain prospects note ;
  The mists that o'er far summits float,
The granite crag at distance viewed ;
  Where man himself but looks a mote,
Amid the Solitude !

The gush of wild-winds as they spring
  Low murmuring round thy heathy side,
A fresher incense seem to bring,
  A purer tone of joy provide ;
  And as along our brow they glide,
Methought in every touch to trace
  A spirit felt, but undescried,
—The Genius of the Place.

What dreams are ours, thus pondering mid
  The Desert all around us spread !
Half seen in light, in shade half hid,
  Dusk vales below, rocks overhead ;
  And where the cataract flashing dread
Boils up in its tremendous glee,—
  By the blithe crowd unvisited,
—Yet sought and loved by me." *

* *On Longaford Tor*, from *Castalian Hours*, by Sophie Dixon.

H

Miss Dixon wrote many poems on subjects of interest connected with Dartmoor, all breathing of love for the " old, wild forest," and her descriptions of the scenery are exceedingly faithful and full of poetry. Two interesting works, consisting of Journals of Excursions on the borders of Dartmoor, also emanated from her pen, and were published at Plymouth, in 1830. She was born at Plymouth, but for some time made the moor her home, her delight, as evinced by her writings, being to wander over its wild hills. The preface to her book, *Castalian Hours*, is dated from Dartmoor, the 18th December, 1828; her death occurred in 1855.

Descending the steep sides of Longaford Tor we pursued a northerly course, and passing Higher White Tor,* we reached the wild stretch of boggy land known to the moor-men as Row Tor. Row Tor itself is further to the westward, and why this name is given to this portion of moor, I am unable to say. It is comprised between the upper waters of the East and West Dart and the new-take wall that runs along the hill side behind Archerton and the powder mills. The greatest part of it is very boggy, and it is of an extremely wild and desolate character, though its solitudes have been at some time invaded, for vestiges of ancient operations are not wanting on Row Tor. Now, however, it is for-saken, and in the worst of its miry spots is shunned by the cattle that range the moor. I remember on one occasion, when making my way over the northern portion of this boggy tract, from the East Dart below Cut Hill to the valley of the West Dart, starting a fox in the middle of the bog, and

---

* Often called Whitten Tor.

to observe the way he made off over the miry ground, on which I was obliged to tread with the greatest of care, made me quite envious of his powers of getting over such rough country.

I have mentioned the new-take wall that runs behind Archerton and the powder mills, which brings to my recollection a curious accident which befel a Dartmoor man of my acquaintance, in climbing over it. He related the circumstance to me, several years ago, when we were seated one afternoon in a combe called Deep Swincombe, near to a little mining hut, which I had been examining, similar in construction to the one I have mentioned as existing on the Erme, near Staldon Barrow. There is a curious trough in front of it, which was used in all probability for purposes connected with the preparation of the ore, but the moor-men around will not see anything other in it than a feeding trough, and in the hut nothing more than a stye, and as a consequence the little hut is locally known as the "pigs' house." From our position near it we could look across the moor, and see the new-take wall behind the powder mills, some four miles distant, and in the course of our conversation my Dartmoor friend mentioned the circumstance in question. It seems he was returning homeward one day, when, in attempting to climb the wall, one of his fingers by some means got jammed between two stones, and it was in vain that he endeavoured to free himself. Having only one hand at liberty he was unable to move the stones, and though he pulled with all the force at his command he could not extricate his hand. At length believing he was really caught fast, and knowing that it was useless to think of waiting until any person might happen to pass that way, he pulled out his knife with the intention of releasing himself by severing his finger. While quite determined upon performing this surgical operation upon himself, our friend was, of course, in no violent hurry about it, and thought he might as well make one more effort for freedom before resorting to such an extreme measure. Accordingly there was more pulling and tugging at the unlucky member, this time, fortunately, with success, and our Dartmoor friend came out of his unpleasant predicament with no worse injury than a very sore finger.

I venture to think my readers will not be inclined so much to pity this unfortunate wight, as to look upon his accident as a retribution, when they learn that he was no other than the self-confessed despoiler of the old bridge at Bellaford.

It must, of course, have been between very large stones that the finger was caught, otherwise it would have been no difficult matter to have toppled a portion of the wall over, and so have freed the hand. As a rule, however, these new-take walls are composed of stones of no great size, and these being of rough, uneven shape, they do not lay closely together, so that it is not generally a hard task to move them from their position. But there are some walls on Dartmoor the stones in which are of an exceedingly large size, and of such no better examples are to be found than those constructed by John Bishop of Swincombe. By the side of the Ashburton Road, between Two Bridges and the Cherrybrook, may be seen one of his buildings, the stones, or rather blocks, composing it, being very large indeed, and of good shape, so that an exceedingly regular piece of building has been produced, quite different to the generality of these new-take walls.

No mortar is ever used, the stones simply being piled one upon the other, and grey and weather-stained as they are, their appearance is thoroughly in keeping with their rugged surroundings. Some of these walls have been standing for a very long period.

After rambling over a portion of the wild district of Row Tor we found ourselves at the head of the Cherrybrook, and here, sitting down by the little stream, we were once more fain to open our wallets, and satisfy the hunger which had been created by the keen air of the hills. It was now drawing on to the close of the afternoon, and since the morning the day had been all that we could desire for the purpose of our ramble, but as we sat resting ourselves by the brookside, we were aware of a rapidly impending change. A death-like stillness suddenly seemed to rest upon all around, a quiet which was not a calm, and which had something almost unearthly in it. A gloom, too, spread itself with great rapidity over the face of nature, the clouds rolling up and speedily obscuring the sun.

Hastily gathering our impedimenta, we made our way quickly towards the hollow, down which the stream rushes to the north-west of White Tor, but hardly had we gained it when the storm burst in its full fury upon us. First a pattering of big rain drops, and then, apparently at no great distance above our heads, a tremendous peal of thunder. The old moor seemed to tremble beneath the shock, and the hills around echoed and re-echoed the deep roar. Vivid flashes of lightning darted out from the inky clouds, and appeared to strike the dark crags which towered near us, and a drenching rain descended with a loud hissing noise. There was no cessation to the roar of the thunder.

Peal after peal crashed out from the heavens, all nature
seeming as if in the throes of some tremendous struggle.
The storm was almost appalling in its severity, and there
was no place to which we could turn for shelter from its
pitiless fury.

> " Heaven aid that hapless traveller then
>   Who o'er the *Wild* may stray
> For bitter is the moorland storm,
>   And Man is far away." *

We toiled onward through the drenching rain, and as
each lightning flash lit up the moor with a blinding
glare, followed instantly by a sharp report which rolled
around every hill and tor, it was as if the day of doom was
at hand. There was a grandeur and an awfulness in the
scene which was most impressive, and exposed as we were to
the full violence of the storm, and thoughts of our safety
being naturally paramount with us, yet could we not restrain
a certain fearsome admiration of the wild battle of the
elements. It was an experience never to be forgotten, the
artillery of heaven seeming to be arrayed against, and as
with a desire of annihilating the grim tors of the moor.

The Cherrybrook rose rapidly, the rain descending in perfect sheets of water, and the ground at the bottom of the
hollow was soaked to such an extent that we could proceed
but very slowly. But we made the best of our way onward,
splashing over the boggy ground, and drenched to the skin,
the storm continuing to rage all the time with unabated fury.

On drawing near the water-course—or leat—which
supplies the powder mills, we saw that it had overflowed its
banks, and the little bridge formed of granite stones laid

---

* Carrington. Ballad of *Childe the Hunter.*

across it, and which was in our track, was not to be seen, being entirely covered by the swollen stream. This was now so turbid that it was seemingly impossible to discover where the bridge was, but knowing its situation I waded into the water, and feeling about with my staff at last found it, and looking carefully down, could just discern it beneath the dark brown stream. I had to be very cautious in my movements, for the banks being under water, a false step would have plunged me into the leat. Carefully noting the position of the bridge, I returned to the spot where I had left my wife, and lifting her in my arms, again waded towards it, and made my way slowly across, landing safely on the opposite side.

By this time the storm had somewhat lessened, although the rain still continued to descend furiously, but as we plodded on it gradually moderated. At length we gained the Princetown and Moreton road, and entered on the new-takes, on the opposite side, our design being to make for Dunnabridge Pound, where we should strike the road to Dartmeet. Across these we pursued our way, as quickly as the state of the ground and our drenched condition would permit, and on reaching Dunnabridge were glad to have firm ground under our feet once more.

During the remainder of our journey we had a good road, and before we reached Hexworthy the storm had entirely ceased, the sun, though now declining, again sending forth its smiling beams. The good old sheep-dog—Help,—a great favourite with us, and an occasional companion of ours in our rambles, met us at the door, and welcomed our return with a joyful wag—or rather, with an attempt at such—of his short stump of a tail. A change of clothing, and a good

fire, soon made us comfortable again; and we sat down to
the appetizing cheer which was quickly prepared for us,
none the worse for our exposure to a Dartmoor thunder storm.

CHAPTER VII.

A RAMBLE TO EAST DART HEAD.

WITH bright anticipations of a pleasant ramble amid some of the wildest and most desolate scenery of Dartmoor, I set out one fine morning in the summer of the same year as that of the adventure related in the previous chapter, with my wife and our little companion Snap, on a long day's tramp to the source of the East Dart and the Cranmere morasses.

What pleasing expectations does the contemplation of a jaunt of this sort call forth. To climb to the tops of some of the giant hills, and gaze upon the varied and beautiful prospects observable from their lofty summits,—to watch the cloud shadows chasing one another over the brown hillsides,—to linger beside some brawling brook, and watch its tiny ripples as it onward flows, and listen to its never-ceasing music,—to wander amid the deep combes by the remains of the old tin seeker of former days,—to stroll through a long deserted hut village where nothing now is left to tell of its former existence, but the foundations of the walls lying among scattered boulders of granite,—to stray where the columnar circle or kistvaen bring before our mental vision the inhabitants of the wild moor in the far away times of antiquity,—raises in the breast of the lover of this great

Devonshire desert feelings of delight indeed, and in its invigorating breezes how light and elastic are his spirits as he wanders over its lofty ridges, and how free, how happy, is everything around.

Our way first led us to Dunnabridge Pound, from whence we walked across the new-takes, where is a good track by the side of the walls, to Bellaford Tor, and from that fine old pile, not aiming at taking the shortest route, we proceeded across Lakehead Hill to Post Bridge. After a short sojourn there we followed a track that leads for some distance up the western bank of the Dart, and on reaching the foot of Broad Down, around which the river makes a great sweep to the eastward, we forsook the stream and ascended the hill, which is here very precipitous.

On its crest are the remains of an ancient village enclosure, the wall of which has, unfortunately, been considerably despoiled by those who found in it a convenient quarry when forming the new-take in which it is now situated. We had made a thorough examination of this interesting relic of antiquity some short time previously, so did not linger long within its vallum now, but clambering over the new-take wall, which has actually been constructed on the line of a portion of the ancient rampart, found ourselves on the open forest.

We now took a somewhat northerly course towards the river, which we struck at the head of a hollow formed by the abrupt declivity of Broad Down on one side, and by the steep slopes at the foot of the high ground which stretches down from Siddaford Tor, on the other. Down this hollow a very pleasing peep is obtainable, which though not by any means extensive, enables one to see one or two attractive objects, and the spot we viewed it from being closed in by high ground this little peep served to relieve the monotony of the scene.

Proceeding a short distance up the river we reached a very charming cascade; it is not of great height, but is interesting, and its situation in this wild and deserted spot renders it peculiarly attractive. A ledge of rocks stands in the channel, over which the stream falls, and amid the numerous boulders lying in its way, it winds and twists in its impetuous haste to hurry forward on its course. The river although not swollen by rains was yet not lessened in its usual volume by drought, so that the beauty of this solitary fall was not impaired.

After lingering for a short time at this spot, we proceeded up the stream, following one of the numerous sheep tracks which are here on its western bank. Not far above, the steep banks gradually recede from the river, forming a level, grassy hollow, through which the Dart meanders, and at its upper end contract again, their sides rising rocky and precipitous. The opening between them is very narrow, and forms a pass which extends for some distance, and by which access is gained to Broad Marsh, a long valley surrounded by very boggy land, and overlooked by the dreary eminence known as Cut Hill. Through this pass the Dart descends, there being just sufficient room in it for the river and for walking carefully along on its western bank. From the quantity of sand which is washed up on the banks of the stream in the hollow at the foot of the pass, the place is known to the few who are acquainted with it as Sandy Hole.

We have at this spot most interesting remains of the works of the tinners of Dartmoor, and vestiges of their

operations may be seen for some distance up the stream. I
have already briefly described some which exist on the Avon
and the Erme, but they may be seen on every river of Dartmoor. From very early ages its valleys have been worked for
tin, which was obtained by a process known as streaming, the
water from the rivers being diverted over the surrounding
surface, the soil was washed away, leaving the tin behind
to be gathered up by the miners.

So numerous are these stream works that it is impossible to pass through any of the valleys of the moor—or
bottoms, as they are there termed—without meeting with
many of them, not a single spot where surface tin was
likely to be met with having been left undisturbed. They
take the appearance of numberless heaps of stones piled up
with some degree of regularity their sides being formed in
the manner of rough walls, and are always found close to
the rivers or brooks, sometimes extending for considerable
distances along their banks. Remains of old water-
courses, too, will frequently be seen, and ruins of numbers
of the small oblong buildings, some of which I have already
described to the reader; indeed, so numerous are these
latter, that I am acquainted with streams whose course on
the moor is not more than six or seven miles, upon whose
banks I have discovered the dilapidated walls of more than
a dozen of such little buildings. Some were used probably
as temporary dwellings by the miners, and others for various purposes connected with their work, the larger ones—
such as that near Heng Lake on the Avon, and at Stoney
Bottom on the Erme, already mentioned in this work—bearing un-mistakeable signs of being old smelting, or blowing
houses. In Cornwall these little erections were commonly

known as Jews' houses, but the term is not usually applied to them on Dartmoor. The remains in and about the blowing houses are very interesting, and in the course of my explorations on the moor I have spent a good deal of time in their examination, taking measurements and recording a full description of them.

The vestiges of mining operations at Sandy Hole are, however, of more than ordinary interest. The Dart during the whole of its course through the gorge is confined between walls, its banks having been faced by the miners with large moor-stone blocks, and its channel is much narrowed. This has been done in order to confine the waters, and an immense amount of labour must have been bestowed upon the work. The gorge is an exceedingly romantic spot, and, from its remote situation, but very little known.

As we approached its upper end a totally different part of the moor came into view. A long, low stretch of ground, through which the course of the Dart lays, and which is known as Broad Marsh, met the eye, the rising ground on each side of it consisting of nothing but bog, and at the higher extremity the lonely eminence of Cut Hill shutting out all further view. It is indeed a scene of desolate loneliness, the spot being the wildest in the east quarter of the forest. Nothing of life is to be observed wherever the eye may turn; a vast sea of bog stretches far around, nature wears a weird, deserted look, and an oppressive silence rests upon the dreary desert.

Just after leaving the gorge we halted for a short time in order to take the measurements of one of the small buildings to which I have just been referring. It stands close to the river, on its western bank, and I found it to be twenty-three feet in length, and seven and a half feet wide, the ruined walls standing about four feet high. The doorway, as usual, (for these huts are all constructed on one plan) is in one of the longer walls near the corner, though not in that facing the river, but looking towards the western side of Broad Marsh, where the principal mining operations seem to have been conducted. I am acquainted with several other of these houses in this valley.

The works at Broad Marsh present a somewhat different appearance to the generality of the remains of streaming operations in other parts of the moor, the soil seeming to be of a more gravelly, sandy nature. That a great portion of the sand which is now lying on the banks of the river below the pass, and which gives name to Sandy Hole, was washed down from Broad Marsh is most probable, and when we consider the quantity which the various streams must have brought down from the moor when such a number of works were in operation there, we can well understand why complaints were made against the tinners, in the sixteenth century, of causing injury to the harbours by these deposits.

The seeker after tin was most indefatigable, for he has penetrated into Dartmoor's inmost recesses in his search for the metal. Here, not far from the bogs of Cranmere, his traces are to be seen, and no matter how remote the valley, there, though sometimes overgrown with moss, and not very plainly distinguishable, the vestiges of his operations are to be met with. It is generally supposed that the district immediately surrounding Cranmere bears no impress of the former presence of man, and without a careful search around its dreary bogs—which, perhaps, few would care to make—such traces are certainly undiscoverable. But in my explorations in this desolate region I have been able to find that the tinner did not entirely shun it, but that here and there on the long and dreary stretches of boggy land his presence in days gone by is indicated, the wild swamps of this remote portion of the great moor proving no barrier to the quest for the riches which lay among the gravels.

About mid-way up Broad Marsh we halted by the banks of the Dart, which here s but a small stream, and in a little clatter of rocks, wher a bush or to growing from the clefts overhangs the water, we sat ourselves down to rest. An intense stillness reigned upon the moor, bringing vividly to our minds the fact that we were here far removed from any human beings. Indeed so solitary were our surroundings, that the stream and the bushes seemed almost like companions to us in the midst of that desert waste.

After having sufficiently rested ourselves, we resumed our journey up the valley, and soon reached nearly to the head of Broad Marsh, where the river makes a turn, (to the right in ascending) and where a small tributary falls into it. This little feeder takes its rise at the foot of Cut Hill, issuing out of a black, swampy, almost uncanny looking place; a hollow filled with bog from which the stream oozes in a slow, lifeless sort of way. Proceeding a short distance up the Dart, we made a detour, leaving that stream a little on our right, and going up over the rough ground that rises towards Cut Hill. There is absolutely no walking over it; all progression must be made by scrambling and climbing. The ground, which for many feet deep is nothing but black peat of a soapy consistency, is rent into chasms running in every direction, and the surface is thus divided into small islands, as it were, covered with a coarse grass, which from its total dissimilarity to any kind of herbage seen in or near cultivated country, or even in the more accessible portions of Dartmoor itself, gives to the face of nature a strange and indescribable appearance.

This boggy land, which is very elevated, stretches for several miles, covering a considerable area, in which the Dart, the Tavy, the West Ockment and the Taw take their rise, It is altogether as desolate a region as one can well imagine, and cannot fail to impress him who seeks its solitudes. There is a grandeur about these wild portions of the forest, where nature still reigns with undisputed sway; where the eye ranges far around but sees no signs of cultivation or the handiwork of man; where the grim old desert wears the same face to-day as it did ages ago, and where the few birds that make the wilderness their home, bend their flight across the waving grasses undisturbed by the presence of man.

Making once more to the river, after our toilsome progress, we pursued our way along its bank, where is firm ground. It was now little more than a rivulet, for we were nearing its source, which is in a heathery little amphitheatre, surrounded by the dreary bog lands just described. This we at length reached, and choosing a comfortable spot where we might rest, and where a granite block served as an admirable back to our seat, we set out the provisions which we had brought with us, and which Snap appeared not at all sorry to see. This little spot I have made my resting place on several occasions since, and have christened it my Chair. As I have already hinted, I have many little resting places on the moor, to which I have given names, and when passing near one in my rambles, and desiring a halt, I make my way to it.

The head springs of the Dart* lay around where we sat, and one little rill ran tinkling along at no great distance off. As we reclined, enjoying our rest, we amused ourselves by following in fancy the river's varied course. We saw it as it gained in volume, gliding down through the romantic gorge up which we had passed but recently, and tumbling over the rocks below. Then by Lade Hill and beneath Hartland Tor we saw it pursue its course, and so to Post Bridge, near which place it meets for the first time with the signs of cultivation. Still onward to Bellaford Bridge and down Loughter Hole, rushing and foaming along its rocky channel, in imagination we saw it sweep, till at Brimpts Corner the Wellabrook, coming tumbling down by Sherwill, augmented its waters, and the swift stream rolled onward to glide beneath the bridge at Dartmeet and unite with its sister stream. The noble river then pursues its way down a romantic valley, between Holne Moor and the commons belonging to Widecombe, and reaching New Bridge soon leaves Dartmoor. Below this its course lays amid scenery of a more sylvan kind, for joined by the Webburn, it enters the beautiful vale formed by Holne Chase on the one hand, and Buckland Woods on the other. Flowing below Hembury Castle, an ancient hill fort, in the parish of Buckfastleigh, it passes the little town of that name, and after being joined by the Dean Burn, courses onwards to Staverton, passing beneath several fine bridges. Below the weir at

---

* The source of the West Dart is some two-and-a-half miles distant, the land between being but one expanse of bog.

I

Totnes, and where it is joined by the tidal waters, this river receives the Hems, a small stream that gives name to Broadhempston, and below Totnes Bridge it becomes navigable. Its course is still through most fine scenery, which has earned for it the title of the English Rhine, and the many boats which ply upon its waters, afford the tourist ample opportunities of becoming acquainted with this portion of the charming river. Opposite Duncannon it receives yet another Dartmoor stream,—the Harbourn,—which rises on the borders of the moor, between Brent and Dean, and so on by Stoke Gabriel and Dittisham, amid a land of golden grain and summer fruits, its peaceful waters run, till the old town of Dartmouth is reached, and the noble stream renders its tribute to the mighty ocean.

Rising from our place of rest I struck out over the bogs in the direction of Cranmere Pool. The afternoon was now far advanced, so there was not much time to spend in these dreary morasses, and as I have noticed the pool in a subsequent chapter, I will not enter upon a description of it now. Our homeward course was made by way of Teign Head, for having had sufficient of the bogs for one day, on setting out on the return journey, I avoided them as far as it was possible to do, and made my way by some fairly hard ground in the direction of White Horse Hill. On gaining the enclosures of Teign Head we entered them and descended by a little feeder of the Teign, to the westward of the farmhouse. Soon after we crossed the upper waters of the river itself, and made for Siddaford Tor, on gaining which we rested for a little time, enjoying the while the noble panorama of moorland which is unfolded from its crest.

On the summit of Siddaford Tor is a logan stone, one of

the many naturally poised rocks found on Dartmoor which may be rocked on pressure being applied to them, and which those who are tainted with Druidophobia are wont to regard as being artificially placed. The tor is not of great size, but is yet a prominent object from many points on Dartmoor, and is well worth a visit. The stone circles known as the Grey Wethers are situated on the slope below it, and possess an interest for all antiquaries. These circles we passed, and had now a grassy path, marked out by a stone being placed here and there, which was known to both of us, and so made our way over Woodridge Hill to Standon, from whence a track leads to the road at Post Bridge.

Here we were glad to rest in the inn, our walk having been a most fatiguing one, but as it was getting late we did not stay for any length of time. The sun was nearly setting as we left the little moorland settlement on our homeward walk to Hexworthy, and as we passed up over Lakehead Hill and by Bellaford Tor the shadows were deepening over the old moor, and the cry of Dart came up from the valley below. Pushing on by Dunnabridge and back over the road by which we had come in the morning, we at length turned down through Huccaby, and making our way up the hill on the opposite side of the river, were soon rewarded by the welcome sight of the open door at home, and entering quickly found the rest and refreshment we needed.

Ours had been a long day's walk—not less than five-and-twenty miles, and this my wife had accomplished without once showing a sign of flagging,—a very creditable exploit for a lady. A good part of our journey, too, as the reader will have seen, had been over very rough and fatiguing ground,--some of the most difficult to travel over in all

Dartmoor. Snap, our true little companion, and who accompanied us on many a ramble, seemed glad to get home, too, for his journey had been far longer than ours, and how many miles he had travelled that day, it would be quite impossible to say. He was a most daring little fellow, brought up on the moor, thoroughly hardy, and a splendid dog for rabbiting. I have known him, too, to seize a snake, of which there are many on the moor, and by one bite across its back render it incapable of moving, when it was easy to dispatch it. Not many months after his run with us this day to Dart Head, he was accidentally killed, and we both very sincerely regretted the loss of our little Dartmoor companion.

His place was supplied by another terrier, which we had as a puppy a few months after losing our faithful friend, and whom we christened Snap after him. He, too, became in time a Dartmoor wanderer, and often has he sallied forth with us from Hexworthy, on a ramble amid the tors and by the streams of the forest. We had him not quite six years, when he also met his death, and now lies by the side of our first Dartmoor pet.

That night, it is scarcely necessary to say, we slept well, and—though I am not certain about it—I am afraid we were not down particularly early the next morning. But be that as it may, this I can affirm, we were very soon ready to contemplate a fresh ramble over the breezy hills of Dartmoor.

CHAPTER VIII.

A DARTMOOR MIST.

ONE of the dangers to which the Dartmoor wanderer is liable is the sudden arising of those thick mists, so frequent there and enveloping every object in so impenetrable a shroud, that unless he be well acquainted with the moor, it is impossible for him to find his way. And even if the moor is known to him there is often great difficulty in accomplishing this, for he his apt to be misled by the strange appearance that even familiar objects seem to wear, so distorted do they become. It is only when his knowledge is sufficient to enable him to tell where he is by observing the formation of the ground over which he is passing that there is any chance of making his way through it.

Strangers who have never experienced a real Dartmoor mist are apt to imagine that a map and a compass are all that are required to enable one to make one's way across the trackless waste. These, it is true, are accompaniments which no one unacquainted with the moor should neglect to be provided with when venturing to explore its more remote parts, and certainly by pursuing as straight a course as is possible with their aid the confines of the moor may be reached. But it is equally sure that after having gained them he will not find himself at the place which he hoped to arrive at. Bogs, mires, turf-ties, and other impediments to a straight course are constantly presenting themselves, compelling the traveller to frequently turn aside, so it must not be thought that a map and compass will enable one to make a bee line over the moor.

But to one who knows the moor so thoroughly as to be able to ascertain his whereabouts in a mist by noticing the nature of the ground around him, that which might prove an impediment and a stumbling-block to the stranger, is as a beacon light, serving to let him know his exact position, and though the way may yet be not easy, (so thick are these mists that everything around is concealed from view) still he can be in no danger of losing himself entirely.

I have known many instances of people, well acquainted with certain parts of the moor, losing their way in a mist and wandering about in it for hours in the vain endeavour to find their path. To such, a compass (presuming they knew the use of it, which it is scarcely necessary to say but few of the Dartmoor people do) would have proved a ready means of setting them in the right track. The wife of Mr. Hooper, who lives at the little farm at Nun's Cross, went out one evening about six o'clock to fetch in their cows to be milked, and a mist quickly enveloping her, when at no distance from the house, she wandered on the moor until four o'clock the next morning, reaching home in a drenched condition for the driving mists quickly soak one to the skin. By her statement to me she could not have gone far from her house,—not more than a mile or two,—but in vain endeavoured to find her way to it. She got into the valley of the Plym, and came more than once upon the ruins at Eylesborough Mine, and appears to have been wandering in a circle, which is usual with persons lost in a mist. Most people after walking about on the moor a whole night would be glad enough to go to rest without delay on gaining their home, but Mrs. Hooper had purposed going to Loddiswell, near Kingsbridge, the next morning, to see her son, so on arriving at her home she, without loss of time, proceeded to make her butter, as usual, and at six o'clock, it being then clear weather, she set out to walk to Brent across the moor. On arriving at that place and finding she was too late for the train, she walked the extra two miles to Kingsbridge Road, to take the coach to her destination.

Her husband not long afterwards lost himself in a somewhat similar manner, but by following the Plym reached Cadaford Bridge, near which he was able to obtain shelter till the morning.

This plan of following a stream is the very best that anyone who has any doubt about his way, when lost in a mist, can adopt; and though, perhaps, conducting him far from his desired destination, will yet enable him to reach the roads on the confines of the moor.

In chapter IV. I have already made mention of Cadaford Bridge, which carries the road from Meavy to Lee Moor over the Plym, and now, at the risk of being thought guilty of digressing, I venture to briefly notice some attractive objects which are situated not far below it.

From the bridge the stream descends through a wild and romantic valley, the hill on the left hand rising bleak and bare, with scattered granite lying on its slope. On the right hand, about a mile down, the waters leave the foot of the well-known Dewerstone, a picturesque object on the very borders of the moor. The rocks rise abruptly from the river's bank, towering up to a great height, the grey granite being partially hidden by the creeping ivy that clings to it. The river rushes impetuously onward over the boulders with which its channel is filled, and lower down is joined by the Mew, so that the hill on which the Dewerstone is situated is peninsulated by the two streams.

To this fact it, in all probability, owes its name, *dewer* being, there seems to be little doubt, a modernised form of the Celtic *dwr*, which means *water*, (the *w* is pronounced something like *oo*, only with a rather thinner sound) so that the name of the rugged cliff would really mean.the *water stone*, or *stone of the waters*.

Immediately below the confluence the stream is spanned by Shaugh Bridge, the surroundings of which are of a most interesting character, and being within easy reach of Plymouth is much frequented in the summer time by excursionists.

Carrington with true poetic feeling has sung the praises of this charming spot.

> " How oft, as noon
> Unnoticed faded into eve, my feet
> Have linger'd near thy bridge, romantic Shaugh ;
> While, as the sister-waters rush'd beneath,
> Tumultuous, haply glanced the setting beam
> Upon the crest of Dewerstone. The hawk
> Rested upon the aged cliff ;—around
> A holy silence reign'd ;—the mountain's breast
> Lay hush'd as midnight ;—not a vagrant gale
> Sigh'd through the woods of Plym, and on the soul
> Fell deep the impressive calm. The sun-tinged cloud
> Sail'd slowly through the heav'n ; but Earth had nought

BICKLEIGH VALE.

Of motion, save the river hurrying on
To seek the distant billow.   One such hour
Outweighs a year of misery ; and oft,
In the great struggle with the tyrant world,
The spirit feels refresh'd as Memory paints,
In hues imperishable, scenes like those
Which, in that hour of freedom, lay around
My happy path. " *

Below Shaugh Bridge the river hastens towards Bickleigh Vale, whose sylvan shades afford a charming retreat for the lover of the soft and beautiful in nature.   Quite a contrast is it to the wild moor.   Here the river glides onward between thickly wooded slopes, and the rambler pursuing the path along its bank is rewarded by ever-varying scenes of loveliness.

Bickleigh Vale is the subject of a poem by Nathaniel Howard, which was first published in 1804.   The talented author was born at Plymouth, and was for some time resident at Tamerton Foliot—distant from that town about five miles—where he kept a school.   Howard was well versed in the Persian language, and in the first volume of the *Transactions of the Plymouth Institution* (1830) there is a paper by him on *Persian Poetry*, which displays a vast amount of research.   His poem on Bickleigh Vale contains a fine description of that enchanting spot, many of the passages being exceedingly happy, and exhibiting a thorough appreciation of the beauties of nature.

The river courses onward for several miles through this wooded valley, and at length meets with the tidal waters where Saltram's stately trees rise by the broad expanse of

---

* Carrington's *Dartmoor : A Descriptive Poem.*

the Laira, and soon after, where is seated that fair town to which it gives name, is lost in the mighty ocean.

A charming writer has given us some sweet lines which he has named *By the Plym*, and ere taking our leave of the river, I cannot refrain from extracting from the poem the following verse.

"At eve, my tiny darling,
 We'll wander by the Plym,
And hear the happy blackbird
 Pour forth his vesper hymn,
And watch the shadows of the sky
 Upon the water swim,
While homeward fast the black rooks fly
 Where Saltram woods grow dim."*

I have been digressing indeed. I commenced by endeavouring to say something about the moorland mists, and now find myself at the mouth of the Plym. But nothing so natural, gentle reader; for when one gets into a Dartmoor mist there is no saying whither he may wander. I can assure thee I have not strayed from my subject with any intention of *myst-*ifying thee;—rather will I plead guilty to having *missed* my way,—but in good truth I believe the river *carried me away*.

It is surprising how distorted objects will become in these Dartmoor mists, and how confusing is the appearance to the traveller. Small objects, close at hand (and only such as *are* near can been seen at all) look like large ones beheld at a distance. They will sometimes burst upon the sight with almost startling suddenness, and with bewildering effect. I have seen sheep that when first perceived looked like beasts as large as bulls, and with their woolly coats

---

* From *Summer Songs*, by Mortimer Collins, 1860.

reminded one of the mammoths of old, which on getting but a few steps nearer to them at once assumed their natural appearance. I remember on one occasion, when riding slowly in a dense mist down the Abbots' Way near Red Lake, being startled by coming suddenly upon what at first sight appeared to be some huge black Newfoundland dogs, and which at first quite startled me, but what the nearer approach of a few yards showed me to be several rough and shaggy calves of the black Scotch cattle, kept on Harford and Ugborough Moors, and immediately afterwards the cows they were following came into view.

I have had many—very many—experiences of Dartmoor mists, but the most curious illusion I ever remember to have met with happened to me once near Glascombe Bottom, some short distance to the northward of the Eastern Beacon on Ugborough Moor. I was making my way along the slope with a companion, the mist being so thick that one could see but a very short distance, and so penetrating that we were wet through, and feeling cold and chilled, when suddenly I saw looming up through the dull mist what I supposed to be a cottage with several fir trees growing close to it, and my companion also saw it at the same time. I stopped bewildered, not being able to understand where I had got to. I knew how very easy it was to deviate from one's course in such weather, and to gradually swerve round to quite an opposite direction to the one intended to be pursued, and at first thought that I must have done this. But even if such were the case, I could not understand for the life of me where I was, for I knew every inch of the ground, and was positive that there was no such thing as a cottage on the moor anywhere near. Besides the ground I was treading made me feel sure I had not wandered out of my track, but was descending towards the Glaze, according to the route I had decided upon taking when the mist first came on. Yet, there in front of me appeared a cottage as plain as ever I saw anything in my life. My companion, as soon as he sighted it, suggested that we should make towards it, and after looking around me in wonder, I acquiesced. We stepped briskly forward along the slope with this intention, when, lo! as if by the effects of enchantment, the cottage, trees and all, vanished from our sight, and in their place a granite block, not above two feet high, with a straight side and a sloping top, with a tuft of rushes growing beside it, was all that there was to be seen. It could not have been more than about a score of yards distant from us when first we saw it, but looked to us over a hundred. No illusion could be more complete; the walls, the roof, and the trees, all appeared perfectly plain, and had we been strangers to that part, and by any chance passed on our way, it is quite certain we should have believed that we had seen a habitation.

There is not much doubt that natural illusions of this kind have given rise to many of the tales of witchery and enchantment related in connection with the pixies of the moor. These little elves are credited with having performed the most wonderful things, although it is true that the Dartmoor peasant of to-day has somewhat lost faith in their ability to accomplish all that they have been credited with, and can only say that he has " heerd tell " that such was the case. The stories of the stones in the columnar circles having been seen dancing at noon have been considered to owe their origin to a purely natural cause. Objects that are seen through the agitated waves of air arising from the heated surface of the ground assume a quivering motion, and it is this which has doubtless given rise to these superstitions.

The Will-o'-the-Wisp, too, has, no doubt, had a hand in originating some of our Dartmoor superstitions, that which science easily explains having been set down as supernatural.

Towards the close of the year 1878, I remember meeting with a very unpleasant adventure in a mist on the moor. I had left Hexworthy in the forenoon, which was bright and pleasant, and climbed up the hill to Aune Head, from whence, by way of Whitaburrow, I had made for Brent. Here I stayed until about six o'clock, when I set out on my return journey across the moor, though not by the same route as I had chosen in the morning. I now took one which is always used by the farmers and moor-men around Dartmeet, Dunnabridge or Hexworthy, when crossing to Brent, and with which I was perfectly well acquainted. This enters the moor at Dockwell Gate, (called by the country people Dock'ell, or Dockhill) about two and a half miles from the town of Brent,* and passing over a small portion of Brent moor, crosses Dean, Buckfastleigh and Holne moors, and meeting the road close by Cumsdon Tor, enters upon the forest at Saddle Bridge. There is no actual path, but here and there certain natural objects which serve to denote the route.

It was drawing towards dusk when I reached Dockwell Gate, and slightly misty, but only sufficiently so to obscure objects at some distance off. I pushed on over Brent Moor,

---

* Not *village*, gentle reader. Brent, small as it is, is really a market town.

where for a little way we have a green track among the heather, and which I have many a time made my way over at all hours of the day and night, and in about half-an-hour reached a little ford on Dean Moor, from near which a track-line leads direct to the summit of a hill to the north-ward called Pupers—probably a corruption of Pipers. This track-line, like the others upon the moor,—and there are many—consists of a bank of earth and stones, four or five feet in height, and five or six feet in width,* Some are much wider than this, and have been termed trackways and regarded as roads, but, I cannot help thinking, in error. The moor-men always term them reaves, and look upon them as ancient boundaries, which in all probability they are. It is not unlikely that many of them were bounds set up by the tinners of the moor, the question of properly defining the extent of the ground over which each tinner, or company of tinners, had a right to labour, being one that received a great amount of attention, as the laws made by them at their Parliament at Crockern Tor, and which are still extant, attest.

I had now the ascent of the hill before me, which, however, is only gradual, the distance to the top from the little ford referred to being about a mile. Pupers, or Pipers as I have heard it called, possesses two tors upon its summit (doubt-less the two pipers transformed to stone for playing their instruments on the Sabbath, or some other equally heinous offence) which from measurements I have taken, I find to be two hundred and ninety-eight yards apart. On its western slope, amid the rocks with which the hill is strewn, there is

---

* I have traced it for a distance of 2112 yards, when it is lost.

another small tor. The two principal tors, although of no great size, are rather prominent objects, and render Pupers an easily recognizable hill from a great distance around, and more particularly from the south and east. Being a border hill the view from it is varied and extensive, and the ground surrounding it being mostly of a good hard character, it is easily accessible.

It was growing dark as I descended the opposite side of this hill, but as yet the mist had only slightly increased. Between this hill and another, known on the moor as Snowdon, there is a rocky gully called by the moor-men Snowdon Hole, in front of which rises a small rivulet, which trickling down into a hollow forms a mire extending for some distance down the slope. When riding it is necessary to know how to cross this spot, which can only be done at one place,— the entrance to the gully—where a little path, not much more than a foot in width, and oftener than not covered with water, affords the means of passing. Below, the miry ground prevents a passage being made with a horse, and above, the rock strewn hole is equally an obstacle. To the traveller on foot it is not of so much importance about striking the exact spot, for so long as he keeps high enough he will avoid the mire, and if he should not strike the path, he will, at the worst, only be put to the trouble of clambering over the stones.

However, the ground was well-known to me, and though it was now nearly dark, I made my way to the little path and gained the further side of Snowdon Hole all right. Here, the course is along the side of the hill, care being taken not to sink too much toward the bottom. Suddenly the mist, which had hitherto been hanging around the hill tops, descended, and wrapped everything in an impenetrable veil, which added to the darkness warned me to exercise caution. In less than ten minutes I found I had got too low. I knew there was a large patch of ferns growing on the hillside, and the proper route to pursue was above these, while I found myself in the midst of them. To correct this error by turning slightly up the hill again was soon done, but I utterly failed to discover one or two well-known landmarks, in the shape of tiny fording places over little rivulets that drain from the boggy ground above. However I made nothing of this, for I knew I could not be more than a score or two of yards out of my way, but proceeded carefully on through the mist, which was now so thick about me that it was impossible for me to see more than a few steps in advance.

At some short distance further on I had to cross a very wide bottom, with extremely precipitous sides, and through which courses a stream that runs by Combe, a hamlet near Scoriton and falls into the Dart below Buckfastleigh. This combe, like Snowdon Hole, can only be conveniently crossed by horses at one spot, a fording place known on the moor as Hapstead Ford, leading to which a pathway, worn by the ponies of moormen and farmers, runs down the bank on each side. My aim now was to strike the top of this pathway, so as to descend the steep bank in safety, but the thick mist, combined with the growing darkness, made it a matter of impossibilty for me to do other than guess at its position. I had to be exceedingly careful, too, where I trod, because I knew the bank to be so steep—in some places almost perpendicular—that if I approached too near, a single false step might precipitate me down it.

My only assurance that I was going towards it was my thorough knowledge of the ground. Though I could see nothing whatever, I knew I was proceeding in the direction of the combe, but whether I should be fortunate enough to hit upon the pathway to the ford was quite uncertain. I did not, however, feel much anxiety about that, as being on foot it would be easy enough to cross it at any point by exercising care in climbing down the bank; at the same time I wished to strike it if I could, as by so doing I should, of course, know exactly my whereabouts, and be better able to shape my course over Holne Moor, which I had yet to cross before reaching the forest bounds.

Making my way carefully onward I at length reached the edge of the deep combe, but no signs of the pathway could I discover. I stood still for a few moments to consider my position, and at length came to the conclusion that I had kept rather too low down the hill, and that if I made my way with caution along the top of the bank in an upward direction, I should at length strike the path. This I did, walking along for some distance, but without finding what I was in search of. I stopped again, but any examination of my surroundings was quite out of the question. I had gained the combe and that was all I knew, but whether I was above or below the pathway I could not determine. It now seemed to me that if I had been below it when I first gained the edge of the gully I should have come to the pathway by this time, so thinking I had been mistaken and that I was above it after all, I determined to try the bank downwards, which I did for some distance, but with no success.

Rain now began to fall, but the mist continued as thick

as ever. As I proceeded slowly through it down the edge of the bank, a sudden thought struck me. The combe at some distance below where I had aimed at reaching it, I knew turned to the right rather sharply, and a fear lest I had arrived at this portion of it took possesion of me, for I was aware that if I had, and tried to cross it there, I should be going away from home instead of towards it, and I stood still undecided what to do. It was now that a compass would have been of service to me, for by its aid I might have discovered at once whether I really was by this lower portion of the gully or not, but I had none with me. By following the stream that ran through the combe I might have got off the moor, of course, but this was not what I wanted to do. my destination lying quite in the opposite direction. Even this though in the mist and darkness would not have been quite so easy as it may seem, for the stream would have been invisible, and I should have had to feel my way along its banks.

However, I was able to relieve my perplexity by a little reflection. I could only dimly perceive the nature of the bank, it was true, but nevertheless saw enough of it to convince me I had not got to the spot I feared. At the place where the ford is situated, the side of the combe for some distance is high and steep, and by climbing partly down it, and making a careful scrutiny I discovered that it was so at the spot where I was standing. This reassured me, so giving up all thoughts of looking for the path, I cautiously clambered down the remaining portion of the steep side, and reached the bottom. Feeling my way in the darkness, a very few steps brought me to the little stream, which is of no great width, so not staying to search for a convenient spot to cross it, I walked through it, and then making across the bottom of the gully, gained its opposite side, which is not so high as the one I had just descended. Scrambling up this I looked about me for a moment, and then deciding upon my course, struck out, with a hope that I might be able to keep to it, up the ascent before me.

The rain now descended in torrents, blowing into my face, and causing me to keep my head well down. I have sometimes when in a mist on the moor steered by observing the direction the wind is blowing from, which, if it were not liable to shift, might be a good plan enough, but as one, of course, can never be sure about this condition, it is not a safe one. In the present instance it was not even possible for me to adopt this course, so I endeavoured to go as straight as I could without such aid, and at first imagined I was doing so, though it was not very long before I discovered my mistake.

It was now intensely dark, and a most miserable, wretched night. I was drenched to the skin, and as I wandered on through the darkness I tried to cheer myself with the belief that I should shortly see the bright, cozy peat fire on the hearth at home. But soon this hope grew fainter and fainter. I felt convinced I was going in a wrong direction, or I should ere this have hit upon landmarks which I knew. For a long, long time I moved on; where I wandered I cannot tell, but I found it quite impossible to make any real headway.

I stopped at last bewildered, and began to feel weary and weak, and wished that I had made my way to the in-country before crossing the gully. This, however, was worse than useless, so I determined to keep moving, and hoped that I might yet chance upon some object which would enable me to learn my position. Several times I saw what looked like a wide valley before me, the slope of the opposite hill seeming to loom through the mist and darkness, and when first beheld I thought I was looking across the valley of the Wobrook to the hill known as Down Ridge. But this was only an illusion; a small hillock, on rather higher ground, sometimes but a few yards distant, being the object to which the treacherous mist had given the appearance of a hill.

Still the rain beat fast upon me, and the mist and darkness shut out everything around me, as I plodded wearily on, knowing that my only chance was to keep moving. Suddenly the ground seemed to sink beneath my step! and I fell out into the darkness, and went rolling down, down a steep bank, falling breathless upon my back at the bottom. Luckily the bank was overgrown with heather, which broke my fall, so that I sustained no hurt beyond a severe shaking. Laying for a brief space I gradually recovered myself, and then perceived I was at the bottom of a narrow gully. I thought little of my accident then; in fact I may say I almost congratulated myself upon it, for it was the means of showing me where I was. I now knew I was in an old mine working known as Ringleshutts Girt, near to which I should have passed had I been able to have kept to my proper track, for I was aware there were no other such trench in that part of the moor.

Climbing up out of this pit, on the side opposite to which I had fallen, I sat down on the bank to rest, raining as it was. I felt it would be madness to leave this gully, and strike out over the moor. Cumsdon Tor, where I should touch the road, was my next point, but I saw at

once that it would be far better to abandon any attempt at
making a direct course, and to follow these workings. They
would lead me to some ruined mine buildings, where a little
stream, called Wennaford Brook—a tributary of the Dart—
takes its rise, and which I could follow. But I felt exhaust-
ed, and almost sleepy, and a feeling came over me that I
must yet rest awhile before I could pursue my way. Groping
about I discovered some thick tufts of heather growing over
a little hollow on the edge of the bank, and creeping under
them, I laid myself down, and had the rain not been falling
I believe I should have stayed there, so weary did I feel.
I closed my eyes, but quickly found that to remain there in
the pitiless rain, which the heather but very imperfectly
shielded me from, would be sheer madness, so pulling myself
together, I felt my way once more to the bottom of the girt,
and climbed up the other side again, knowing I should have
better ground there. I had to feel my way along its
edge, for to see anything was quite impossible, and so slowly
made my way down by it towards the mine.

On a sudden something white appeared before me. This
I found to be a gravelly path, and knew that I had come
upon an old track. It is called Sandyway, and is to be seen
here and there in its course from Holne Moor to Fox Tor
Mire. This raised my spirits, but soon I lost the track, and
the mist so bewildered me that I scarcely knew what to think.
However, I kept on by the edge of the workings, and at last
I saw to my great joy the tall chimney shaft of old Ringleshutts rising up before me.

I was all right now, though I had still several miles to go
before I could reach home. But I did not mind that, for I
knew I was saved from having to wander about the moor

through the pitiless night. I stopped at the little stream and quenched my thirst, and then debated with myself whether I should follow it to Wennaford Bridge, or whether I should walk back towards Holne Moor Gate by the old mine road, which is a very good, plain track. The former would have been very much the shortest, but I felt that it would be likely to take me quite as long to perform, for it would be no easy task to follow the stream down the rough bottom in the darkness, so I chose the latter. I had to walk almost back to Holne Moor Gate before getting into the road to Hexworthy, but by stepping briskly out, which the knowledge that I was now in a fair way of reaching home encouraged me to do, I soon gained it. Here I stopped by the road-side and pulled off my boots, and emptied them of the water which they contained, after which I set out as quickly as I could for the little settlement, for I had still between three and four miles to go.

I had now a good road across the moor, so had no further difficulties to encounter, though my weary state and the rain and mist combined to make the walk anything but a pleasant journey. But it was all over at last; Hexworthy was reached, and I was once more beneath the hospitable roof of the Forest Inn. I need scarcely tell with what gusto I sat down to the meal which was hastily prepared for me—not staying to take off my wet garments, so hungry was I, but making good work at my trencher, and then getting off speedily to bed.

Of course, I was not expected. As I had not arrived in the evening it was thought that the weather had deterred me from returning, and it was with surprise that my wife and our good host and hostess found me come back in the night. Most unpleasant was my experience, but "all's well that ends well," and if one *will* be a rambler upon the old moor, why one must of course take it in all its humours, and must not expect but what he will, at some time or other, get overtaken by a Dartmoor mist.

CHAPTER IX.

IN the spring of the year 1879, accompanied by my wife, I left the little market town of Moretonhampstead one fine morning, for a few days ramble over some parts of the moor bordering the north quarter of the forest.

We drove first to Chagford, where dismissing our vehicle, we halted for a short time at the Moor Park Hotel, a most convenient house, and a delightful place of sojourn for tourists, and then set forward on foot to Sticklepath. The sun was bright overhead, and the birds were singing in the trees, as though joyful at seeing all around them so fair and lovely, as we passed by Holy Street, and made our way on to Gidleigh Park, to walk through which permission was kindly granted us. This park—or chase—lying on the verge of Dartmoor, is exceedingly interesting and romantic, and we enjoyed our ramble through its sylvan glades, where in old time roamed the antlered monarch of the forest. Large masses of rock stud the slopes, peeping out from between ancient oaks, while the river rushes impetuously onward in its channel below, white flashes of foam being ever and anon observable between the waving boughs of the forest trees.

From this delightful scene, rendered in the bright sunlight of the fresh spring morning more beautiful still, we passed on to Gidleigh Church and Castle. The ruins of the latter are not extensive, but are certainly interesting. There is a lower chamber, and steps by which the upper apartments were reached. It formerly belonged, according to Risdon, to the family of Prouz or Prous, who held possession of it until the reign of Edward II. The old manor house, a substantial building, is close at hand, the castle, in fact, standing within its courtyard.

Just outside the gate is a curious old well by the road-side. It is covered with granite slabs, and being below the level of the road, there are several steps descending to it.

After an examination of these interesting objects we passed on our way, and soon reached the little hamlet of Forder, from whence we walked on to Throwleigh. This place, like Gidleigh, is close to the moor, and one from which many interesting places and objects on the border commons may be visited. We here observed another well, covered also with slabs of granite.

From Throwleigh we passed on to the moor, and proceeded for a short distance across the common to Payne's Bridge, where we halted for a short time by the Blackaton Brook, and had recourse to our wallets. We found, however, that it was not possible to sit very long with any degree of comfort. It was yet early in the season, and the sun had not attained sufficient power to infuse much warmth into the air, and we were soon made aware that lingering about would never do, for the breezes that came down over the shoulder of old Cosdon had something of winter still about them. We therefore resumed our walk, and followed the road which skirts the moor, passing through Ramsleigh, where is a large copper mine, and leaving South Zeal and South Tawton immediately on our right, soon after reached the village of Sticklepath.

Here we took up our quarters at the Devonshire Inn, and after our long walk were glad of an hour or two's rest. We had not come, however, to remain within doors, so when we considered we were sufficiently refreshed, we prepared to make the ascent of Cosdon, a fine border height of Dartmoor, and not far from the village. It is of great extent, and a very prominent object for a long distance around, and was at one time regarded as the highest hill on Dartmoor, but there are several eminences on the moor which are of greater altitude. It was on this hill that in ancient times the forest perambulations were commenced, the perambulators setting out in a southerly direction and returning to Cosdon from the west. On its summit are several very interesting pre-historic remains, and around it also the streamer has not been idle.

This fine hill is sometimes erroneously called Cawsand,—and is so marked in some maps—which has probably been derived from Cosson, a corruption of its true name. That this corruption to Cosson is not a modern innovation, however, is evidenced by the perambulation of 1609, where the hill is distinctly stated to have been then called "Cosdon, al's Cosson," so that this bit of true Devonshire pronunciation has certainly the respectability of antiquity. In the perambulation of 1240 the name is rendered Cosdonne.

Leaving the Devonshire Inn we retraced our steps for a short distance, re-crossing the Taw, which flows near the outskirts of the village, and a little way further on, between the bridge and South Zeal, turned up on our right hand, and speedily gained the commons. The ascent of Cosdon is not a matter of any difficulty, though it is certainly a work of time, but were it indeed a toil the tourist would be more than recompensed for it by the magnificent prospect which gradually opens out as he ascends, and which we, making pauses, turned frequently to contemplate.

When at last the breezy summit was gained, what a vast expanse of moorland lay before us. Hey Tor and Hameldon looked quite near, and many a hill and tor were seen, some of them close at hand, and others far away, their distant forms just seen through openings between nearer eminences. The view in the opposite direction is one of great beauty and variety, for a large tract of North Devon, and a great part of Somerset is in sight. The hills near Barnstaple, and Exmoor are to be distinctly seen, with glimpses of the bright streak of sea that washes the northern coast of our county. It is a truly grand prospect that rewards the visitor to the summit of old Cosdon, should he happen to be fortunate enough to have fine, clear weather; and the antiquities upon its crest will present attractions to those who delight in an examination of the stone remains of the old dwellers of the moor.

Cosdon from its great height and size is observable from many a point on Dartmoor. I am able to see the old hill from an eminence in the parish in which I reside— South Brent,—for, as remarked in Chapter III. it is visible from Western Whitaburrow on Brent Moor, the most southern point of the forest, so that the observer can thus see from one end of it to the other.

Some few years ago a gentleman of my acquaintance, in making the ascent of Cosdon, found a gold watch lying amid the heather. He returned to London, where he resided, shortly after, taking the watch with him. Some months afterwards he took it to a watchmaker for the purpose of having something done to it, and he happening to know the number of the watch was able to help the finder to discover the rightful owner It belonged to a relative of the Rev. C. H. Spurgeon, who, I need scarcely say, was both surprised and pleased at recovering his property in so unexpected a manner.

After examining the antiquities of this hill, we directed our steps towards Taw Marsh, a level space strewn with masses of granite, through which courses the Taw as it comes rushing down from the wild parts of the moor. We followed the stream for some distance, when selecting a suitable place for crossing, we gained the opposite bank, and made our way up the slopes to the Belstone. Tors, which are situated on the summit of the ridge that rises between the Taw and the East Ockment, or Okement.

Another grand view rewarded us for the climb, which after fully enjoying, we descended towards the East Ockment, passing on our way the circle known as the Nine Stones. This circle is in a very complete state, and consists of a greater number of stones than its name indicates, there being really seventeen; they are not, however, of a very great size. A superstition formerly existed in the neighbourhood that these stones were seen to dance every day at noon.

Turning towards Belstone, a little village on the very verge of the moor, we passed onward and descended once more to Sticklepath, where we were glad to rest after our fatigues of the day.

The next morning we were up betimes, for we had planned a long excursion. We first took our way to Okehampton, which is about four miles distant, enjoying the walk in the beautiful morning air. There are many places of interest around this little border town, and it is a very convenient centre for the explorer of northern Dartmoor; there are good hotels there, the principal being the White Hart in the main street, a favourite resort of tourists: the London near the West Bridge is also good.

After spending a short time in the town we took the train for Bridestowe, and on arriving at that station, immediately turned moorwards. We stopped for a short time, for some refreshment, at the Fox and Hounds, a little wayside inn, and then bent our steps to the commons, which are not very far in the rear of the house. On the borders of the moor we saw workmen engaged in constructing the railway which was to be used for the purpose of bringing in peat to the main line, from the works of the Dartmoor Compressed Peat Company, a venture which had but a very short existence, for like the other projects to which I have adverted for making money on Dartmoor, it quickly came to an ignominious end.

Crossing the south slope of Great Nodder, we gained the upper waters of the Lyd, and made our way towards Arms Tor. The Lyd rises to the eastward of Great Nodder, and leaves the moor just before reaching Lydford, and after a course through some very beautiful scenery falls into the Tamar.

Our next point was Great Links Tor, on reaching which we halted, and in a little hollow of the rock, partook of some refreshment, enjoying at the same the pure moorland air, and the wild and romantic scenery surrounding us. This halt at an end, we continued our ramble, passing on by the upper waters of the Rattle Brook to Amicombe Hill, a very lofty ridge, at the foot of which that stream courses on to mingle its waters with the Tavy. Here a wide expanse of the most wild and desolate parts of Dartmoor lay before us. Away to the eastward we could see the dreary brown ridges in the neighbourhood of Cranmere Pool, over which a deep stillness was brooding, and a lifeless aspect seemed to rest.

Proceeding over the northern part of the hill we descended the almost precipitous side to the West Ockment, in the direction of Sandy Ford, one of the forest bounds. Recent rains had considerably swollen the stream, and no boulders which could be used as stepping stones were to be found, but as it happens that whenever I am present, one need never fail in finding a *crossing*, a means of getting over at once presented itself. Taking upon myself the duties of ferryman, I bore my wife across in safety, but at the cost of a wetting for myself the water rising above my knees.

And now one of the most toilsome ascents on the whole of Dartmoor was before us, our next point being the summit of High Wilhayes, the loftiest hill in the South of England. At that time Yes Tor, which is close to High Wilhayes, was considered to be the highest point, its altitude being then stated to be 2050 feet, but the recent ordnance survey has shewn this to be incorrect. According to this survey the real height of Yes Tor is 2027 feet, while that of High

Wilhayes is 2039 feet.* The ascent from the river is more like a mountain climb than any other upon the moor, and it seemed as if we were never going to reach the top. However, perseverance and patience will accomplish most things, and after having imagined for the fifth or sixth time that the summit was nearly gained, we really saw it before us, and tired and breathless with our long climb, at length reached it, glad to rest ourselves, and at the same time to feast our eyes upon the wondrous view which from its lofty crest delights the beholder.

Although a little higher than Yes Tor, High Wilhayes does not command the view to the northward that may be seen from that celebrated hill, Yes Tor standing, as it were, in front of it, and nearer to the confines of the moor. But the prospect as we turned southward and saw the great range of wild and desolate country, extending for many and many a mile, and filling up the whole scene, was grand in the extreme. Great ridges of brown heath, lying silent and deserted by every living thing,—a true wilderness which cannot fail to impress the beholder with its utter loneliness, stretches of bog and heather only relieved here and there by dark and grim piles of rock, is what meets the eye from the summit of High Wilhayes. It is a sight which is nowhere to be seen in any other place in our island than Dartmoor, for while, in our mountainous districts we have hills of much greater altitude, no such scene of solitariness and weird desolation as is spread before the beholder here, is to be found among them.

---

* The survey gives the exact altitude to a decimal part. I have not thought it necessary to do this.

From High Wilhayes our course lay over the flank of Yes
Tor to West Mil Tor, from whence, after spending some
short time amid its rocks, we turned down the hill, and
crossing one of the green tracks which I have referred to in
an earlier chapter, made towards the Black Fen Brook,—
always called on the moor the Black Vain or Black-a-vain,
and rendered by some writers, and on the ordnance map,
Blackaven. This stream falls into the East Ockment, and
another rises very near it, called the Red Fen, or Red-a-vain,
which taking an opposite course empties itself into the
West Ockment.

After making a halt by a little tributary rivulet for the
purpose of partaking of some further refreshment, our walk
having caused us to grow very hungry, we proceeded to the
Black-a-vain, crossing it by an old bridge near an extensive
stream work. No sooner does one find himself in the
valleys and combes of the moor, than he is reminded of the
busy scene which these now silent places must at some time
have presented, for there the old workings of the tinners are
sure to be met with. The old bridge, though not of such
rude construction as that at Post Bridge, or Bellaford, is
nevertheless very interesting, and its complete isolation from
any habitation or signs of cultivation does not diminish this.
It is of precisely similar construction to the other clapper
bridges of the moor, consisting of piers, across which are
laid slabs of granite. There are two openings for the water,
each about four feet or so in width, and the bridge is nearly
eight feet high from the bed of the stream. The centre pier
composed of several layers of granite blocks rudely cut, is
very wide, projecting up stream beyond the side of the
roadway; it is also wedge shaped, in order that it may

present the less resistance to the water. The bridge is much wider than the others found on the moor the roadway being quite of sufficient breadth to permit of two carts crossing at one time. From its lonely situation this old bridge is known to but few outside the immediate neighbourhood, no mention of it ever having been made, so far as I am aware. That it was erected as a means of communication to the tin workings in this part of the moor is not improbable. It stands close by the bounds of the forest.

From this bridge the course of the Black-a-vain is towards the lower enclosures of East Ockment Farm* by the wall of which it flows, meeting the East Ockment river at the corner of them. In this latter part of its course it falls over numerous small ledges of rocks, forming pretty little cascades, by the side of which a grassy track leads to a ford below, known as Cullever Steps. We did not, however, follow this stream, but leaving it on our left hand, struck out for the higher end of East Ockment Farm enclosures, and passing them, crossed over the East Ockment river.

By this time it was getting dusk, and the sky had become very much overcast. During the previous hour or two it had grown very cold, but we had not anticipated that which overtook us now. Hardly, however, had we gained the slope above the bank of the river, when very suddenly large flakes of snow, began to fall and in an exceedingly short time the ground was covered.

---

* I have sometimes heard this farm spoken of as Harter Farm.

There is a road near here which runs out from Belstone to Ock Mine, so striking this we made the best of our way along it, the snow now falling very fast. Soon we passed the Nine Stones (the circle already referred to), standing like sheeted spectres in the midst of the whitened heath, and pushing on as rapidly as possible, quickly reached the moor gate, and gained the village of Belstone, where we were glad to seek shelter in the little hostelry.

Here the good wife, to whom I was not unknown, having visited her house before, made us comfortable, and set before us a real Dartmoor pasty, from which we certainly were not inclined to turn away. While resting ourselves we indulged in chats anent the moor, and passed a pleasant time by the comfortable peat fire.

Belstone, which is but a small village, stands upon the very border of the moor. The little church, its grey and ancient appearance so thoroughly characteristic of our Dartmoor sanctuaries, with its low, but strong and sturdy looking tower, is well adapted to withstand the fury of the fierce winter storms to which it is exposed. On the village green are two upright granite posts about the height of a tall man and a few feet apart. These, so I have been informed, are a portion of the old village stocks, or the ducking stool (the latter probably) so that it seems in former days the refractory ones among the inhabitants of this remote little village were not strangers to that rough and ready mode of punishment.

Finding that there was not much likelihood of a great improvement in the weather, we thought it better to push on for Sticklepath while we could, so taking advantage of a cessation in the fall we bade adieu to the good landlady of the New Inn, and stepped out into the un-inviting looking evening, and made our way quickly through the village. But we had scarcely left it behind us when the snow commenced to fall faster and faster, until it very soon lay to some considerable depth. We were, however, no longer on the moor, but in a lane that leads from Belstone to Sticklepath, and were consequently sheltered to a certain extent. Speeding along as fast as the weather and the state of the road would permit us, we at length reached the latter village, and were soon once more under the roof of the Devonshire Inn.

My plan for the next day was to have roamed up the valley of the Taw to its source, visiting from there Cranmere and some surrounding spots of interest, but as we sat that evening by the comfortable fireside discussing the probability of the weather permitting of this being carried out, I cannot say that we were either of us sanguine about such being the case. And the next day showed that we were not wrong in our forebodings, for a white carpet covered everything around, so there was nothing for it but to remain within doors. However, the time passed pleasantly enough, and the moor was oftener than once my theme of conversation with those at the snug little hostelry.

I was astir early on the following day, but the weather had not greatly improved, though the sun had caused the snow in some places to partially disappear. But it was no day for Dartmoor, so having made a good lunch, we set out once more for Chagford. As we left Sticklepath the clouds gathered and snow again began to fall, but luckily did not continue, and after a long walk, rendered by the partly melted snow, not too pleasant, we crossed the Teign and entered Chagford. Here we were able to take the rest of which we stood in need until the time of the starting of the coach, which set out from the Three Crowns, an ancient and comfortable hotel. Taking our places we soon left Chagford behind and rattled merrily on over the road to Moretonhampstead.

CHAPTER X.

AN ADVENTURE IN THE SNOW.

AT the commencement of the year 1880, in the very depth of the winter, I set out one afternoon, with my wife, to drive from Totnes to Hexworthy. The moor hills were white with snow, but as there was no sign of anything of the sort in the cultivated country, and I had not heard of much having fallen on the moor, I felt under no apprehension about the journey, thinking I should find it of no great depth. We were driving a little four-wheeled pony carriage, and had with us our terrier Snap, the successor to the one that accompanied us in some of the rambles already related in these pages.

We soon got over the seven miles to Buckfastleigh, through which we passed, and drove on to Holne, a distance of about three miles further, and it was not until approaching that place that we saw any snow, but around there we found it lying about an inch or so deep. We stopped for a short time at the inn, and there learnt that it lay to a great depth on the hills, and that there had been no traffic in consequence over the road across Holne Moor for several days. When I announced my intention of going on to Hexworthy I was told that such would be quite impossible, and was strongly urged not to think of attempting it. I knew every inch of the road, and felt that if it was to be passed over at all I could do it, and not wishing to give up my intended visit, I determined I would try whether this could not be effected;—at all events, I said, there could be no harm in my going on and seeing for myself the state of the road, and if there really was no possibility of proceeding, I could but turn back.

Daylight had long since departed, but it was a clear evening, and the whiteness of the ground made every object visible. Getting into our vehicle we left the inn and drove slowly up the hill to the moor gate, and in due time found ourselves out on the commons. For the first half mile or so all was easy, though I could see the snow was getting deeper and deeper, but so crisp was its surface that the carriage wheels sank but slightly into it. Progress, however, was slow, but as we were in no particular hurry to reach our destination we did not mind that.

When we had covered the distance named, nearly all trace of the road had vanished. The highway across Holne Moor is several feet below the level of the common, having banks on each side. But this wide trench was nearly filled up now, and unless I had been thoroughly acquainted with the direction it took, it would have been a matter of no little difficulty for me to have kept in the track. As it was, however, I was able to manage this, and my knowledge of every turn of the road gave me confidence to go on. By and bye the hill leading to Wennaford Bridge was reached, and to descend this I experienced some difficulty. I was compelled to exercise a great deal of caution, for a slip might have occasioned a disaster, and I felt that I must take my time about it, so leading the pony, while my wife held him well back, I managed to reach the bottom in safety.

Crossing Wennaford Bridge we had now to ascend the opposite side of the little valley, and a long pull it is at the best of times. But my trouble was not so much about getting up this hill, as it was about getting down another, —one some mile and a half ahead of us Cumsdon Tor Hill, which is exceedingly steep and very long. Walking by the side of the pony and allowing him to stop and breathe every now and again, we toiled slowly up, the snow seeming to get deeper and deeper. I began to think I had done wrong in not taking the advice of the people at the inn, but determined I would now push on at all events, for having come so far, I did not like the idea of turning back.

Gaining the top of the hill, we paused to look around upon the great wilderness before us, lying wrapped in a white shroud, with a deathlike stillness brooding over it, broken only by sounds like deep sighs, that ever and anon reached our ears, from the river in the valley below. Objects seemed to take strange shapes in that uncertain light, and there was a wierd, uncanny look in everything around us.

The snow was now so deep that the surface of the road lay several feet below us, but all traces of its course were not quite obliterated, notwithstanding. There being ridges on the tops of the banks on each side of the road, I could, by keeping a good look-out, discern its direction, hidden though it was.

Before reaching Cumsdon Tor the road passes close to some deep hollows, the remains of old mine workings, known as Hangman's Pit, and these we were now approaching. This is a comparatively modern appellation, and the name must not be supposed to have any connection with the term Hangman (i.e. Hang maen) which is not infrequently found in place names. It is so called from the circumstance of a moor-man having hanged himself there, which unfortunate occurrence happened rather more than sixty years ago. It seems that he was returning from Brent Fair, and riding a horse which he had taken in exchange for another. As that which he had acquired was of much less value than the one he had parted with, it is supposed, that, not being able to bear up under the mortification this occasioned him, he determined upon taking his life. This he did by hanging himself to one of the small trees which grow from the sides of the deep pit by the road on Holne Moor, and which has ever since been known as Hangman's Pit.

At this place the road is carried along the side of the hill, bending around the top of the wide combe which descends to the Dart, and on nearing it, I saw that the snow had here drifted in such a manner as to render the way, apparently, quite impassable. Here was a dilemma; we were still about a mile and a half from our destination, and it certainly looked as if it would not be possible for us to drive on any further. Fortunately there was no sign of any more snow falling; had such been the case the consequences might indeed have been serious. It was, however, bitterly cold, and a breeze was springing up our clothing seeming to afford us but slight protection from its scorching keenness. It was no use thinking I had made a mistake in attempting to cross the moor under such conditions, or to feel that I was to blame for not having more fully considered the matter before leaving Holne. All that I could do now was to make the best of matters, and not allow myself to indulge in any vain regrets. Push on we must, if there was any possibility of so doing : with the chaise, if that could be taken ; if not, the pony must be unharnessed and led.

Walking forward a short distance to reconnoitre I saw that by the side of the pit, and for some distance beyond, the snow had drifted until it lay in huge heaps across the road. These great barriers seemed effectually to block the way, laying obliquely across it, being several feet in height and also of considerable width. So far the snow over which we had passed had possessed a hard and crisp surface, —had this not been so, of course, we could not have made our way over it at all—and I was glad to find that the surface of these heaps appeared to be equally hard. I was, however, under some apprehension that if I attempted to get the chaise over them the surface might break, with the result, in all probability, that it would be embedded, but I nevertheless determined upon doing so.

I could not quite see how far these heaps of snow extended, but as I knew that a little distance ahead the road again made a turn and took the same direction as that we had hitherto been pursuing, I judged that the drift would not extend beyond the bend. Desiring my wife, who was sitting in the chaise, muffled up, in the endeavour to keep out the biting air, to hold firmly on, and bidding Snap lay quiet, I took the pony's head, and drew him gently towards the first bank. I did not feel much doubt about his accomplishing the task of surmounting it, although it was certainly a formidable obstacle, for he was a plucky little fellow, and I knew would not shirk the attempt. Cheering him on, and holding the rein in my hand, I clambered up the bank of snow, and he bravely drew the chaise up in safety, and as safely pulled it down on the opposite side, I firmly holding him back as he descended.

We were now in a trench, so to speak, the banks being only a few yards distant from each other. As they had drifted across the road obliquely and not at right angles to it, I could not attempt the second bank from where we landed, but was obliged to draw the pony a length or so along the bottom of the trench, and then partly turn him so as to face the heap squarely. I did not lose any time about it, for I felt it was a somewhat perilous position to be in, and was anxious to clear the drift as quickly as I possibly could; I also thought it was better to keep the pony at his task, than allow him to halt long between the snow banks.

In this manner, therefore, we went on, the chaise being dragged up and down, but piloted as carefully as I could manage it, and at length we cleared the drift. I had one guide, as I passed through it, as to the exact position of the road beneath us, and that was the Wheal Emma Mine leat, which flows under the road, and for a short distance along its side, near Hangman's Pit, and whose channel deep down between banks of snow I could discern.

After stopping for a brief space to give our gallant little steed a breathing time we resumed our journey. Cumsdon Tor Hill was now before us, and this I could not help feeling rather doubtful about. If I could only get to the bottom in safety, the rest, I hoped and believed, would be comparatively easy, unless indeed any drifts in the valley might block the road in a similar manner to those we had just passed through. The dark sides of the rocks of Cumsdon Tor stood out conspicuously amid the snow, and after passing them the descent of the hill commenced.

I got out once more, and with my hand upon the rein, walked by the pony's head. The position of the road was indicated here and there by the banks which in some places were higher than usual. But it was only faintly that its course was thus marked out upon the white expanse which lay below us, very steep and seemingly dangerous to descend. And that it was dangerous the advance of a few yards more convinced me, for the surface affording no foothold for the pony, on reaching the steeper part of the hill, it seemed not unlikely that the animal with the chaise would go sliding off to the bottom of the valley. I therefore immediately stopped, and assisting my wife to alight, placed her at the back of the chaise, with instructions to hold firmly on, but rather to endeavour to pull it back than to lean her weight upon it. Our little Snap, who for a portion of the time had remained in the carriage,—much against his will, though,—followed after, for he had leapt on to the snow as soon as my wife left the chaise. Then seeing that the break was firmly on, I went to the pony's head once more, and placing myself in front of him and facing him, held a rein firmly in each hand close to the bit, and step by step descended the hill, walking backwards and exerting all my strength to hold the pony up. I had to dig my feet into the snow at each step I took before I could obtain a hold in it, and this loosening of the surface helped in some measure to give a surer foothold for the pony as well.

But it was very slow work, for the hill is a long one, and at intervals we were obliged to stop and rest. About midway down my wife's hat blew off, for there was now a rather stiff breeze, and went spinning away over the snow. Being a black one we could watch it as it rapidly descended the side of the hill towards the Wobrook, but no thoughts of attempting to go after it entered my mind, for I dared not leave the pony. The next day, however, John Cleave, guided by my description of the spot near which I last saw it, was able to recover it.

Proceeding carefully down in the manner I have described, the pony having great difficulty in keeping on his legs, we at length reached the bottom of the hill, and crossing Saddle Bridge, entered within the bounds of the forest. Fortunately there were no drifts here, and the rest of our way I now felt very little anxiety about accomplishing. I was within such a distance of our destination that I should soon be able to obtain help if such were necessary, and that there might be a possibility of the snow having drifted between the new-take walls which we had shortly to pass through, I could not but admit to myself. However, we passed on in safety, and with a little care in descending the steep pinch that leads down to the Forest Inn, reached that much desired haven at last, thankful for such a happy termination to our drive over the snow.

A light in the window showed us that the good folks had not yet retired to rest, so knocking at the door, we were soon pleased at beholding the form of Mr. Cleave, with astonishment depicted on his countenance at seeing visitors at such an hour and under such circumstances. He was wearing his spectacles, but as soon as he heard my voice, he lifted them upon his forehead and peered out at us, as if imagining his ears had played him false he felt constrained to doubt his glasses also, and it still remains a saying with us out there, that "master must take off his spectacles before he can see." I am unable to express the surprise with which the good people beheld us, or the warm welcome which was extended to us.

No one had passed over the road for days, and it had been considered impossible so to do. Mr. Cleave had been wanting to go to Ashburton, for it seems his supply of ale had run short, and he was desirous of replenishing his stock, but he had not imagined he could pass with a vehicle over the moor. However, our appearance was, of course, convincing proof that it was to be done, and he announced then and there his intention of attempting it on the morrow, "for" said he, "if you can do it, why, of course, I can."

He did do it, but the good folks of Hexworthy never got their beer the next night, for all that. He crossed the moor safely and reached Ashburton, where he obtained his supply of John Barleycorn, but on the return journey, a snow storm coming on, his cart broke down on Holne Chase Hill, and he was obliged to abandon it.

The cozy peat fire soon restored us to something like comfort, and a hearty repast was not long in being prepared for us; then we gathered once more round the hearth, (but not before I had walked over to Gobbet to call a neighbour to join our circle) and spent a pleasant hour or two before retiring to rest. Little Snap appeared to enjoy the comfort of the fireside as much as any of us, and made himself quite at home. He did not know a great deal of Hexworthy or the moor then, for he was only a puppy about eight or nine months old, but he had plenty of opportunities of becoming well acquainted with Dartmoor afterwards, and in time became a thorough moorland ranger, accompanying me in all my expeditions.

The exposure to the cold air for so long a time had been most wearying, and when the hour came for us to retire, we felt by no means reluctant to yield ourselves up to " Nature's soft nurse."

I should not have attempted this journey had I been aware of the amount of snow upon the moor. It was certainly a risk to run, and had another fall taken place the consequences might have been exceedingly serious, for it would have been utterly impossible for us to have made any haste in order to escape it. But as we came to no harm, we can now contemplate our ride over the snow, if not with pleasure, at least with no feelings of regret at having ventured upon it, though at the same time being far from desirous of encountering another such adventure on Dartmoor.

CHAPTER XI.

CRANMERE POOL.

THE many unsuccessful searches for Cranmere Pool have caused a kind of mystery to attach to it, its position in the midst of bogs rendering it somewhat difficult of approach, and proving a barrier to its being readily discovered. Tourists desirous of seeing the more wild and desolate parts of Dartmoor, sometimes visit it during summer, but to very few of the inhabitants of the moor is it known except by name, and in winter remains un-visited for months together. I have myself conducted men there who were born upon Dartmoor and had lived on it all their lives, but who had never seen the wondrous pool,—in fact had never crossed the north quarter of the forest before. I am well acquainted with it, and can approach, by several ways through the bogs, to within a short distance of it with ease. I have referred to it in my account of the ramble to East Dart Head, to which it lays very near, but thought it more convenient to describe it in the present chapter, and by conducting the reader to it from another direction, be able to give at the same time a brief account of some interesting objects which are passed on the route.

It was a bright morning in the summer of 1881 when I set out with a companion from the town of Moreton-hampstead for a ramble on the moor, with the intention of visiting Craumere Pool in the course of our wanderings. My companion had never been on the north quarter before, and I was anxious to show him some objects of interest there, so not desirous of losing any time, we stepped out briskly towards the moor. This we entered at the gate near Metherell, a farm just on its borders, and proceeded towards Fernworthy, to which a road leads. We did not, however, keep to this, but made a detour to the south of it, and wending round regained it where it crosses the South Teign, and not very far from Fernworthy farmhouse.

Close to this bridge, which is a modern erection, is an old clapper bridge, consisting of one immense stone, which I found to measure ten feet four inches in length, having a width of three feet ten inches, and a thickness of about a foot. The buttresses, which are rather high, are built of rough, un-hewn stones. It is very interesting, and a good specimen of a single-stone clapper.

Passing on we soon reached Fernworthy, an ancient moor farm, lying just within the bounds of the forest, and in its east quarter. In the perambulation of 1609 the name occurs, for we find mention of " ffernworthie hedges," but the present house is probably an erection of some seventy years later. By its grey old walls grow some fine trees, affording in summer a cool and grateful shade, when the noonday sun blazes full upon the hot and thirsty heath.

> " Long years have passed, since he who made his home
> Here by the rocky stream, first raised thy walls :
> Long years have passed ; and out amid the stir
> Of the great world hath many a storm swept by." *

---

* Richard John King. *The Hill Farm.*

Leaving Fernworthy behind us we passed through the gate at the top of the lane that runs by the house, and emerged once more upon the commons, shortly reaching the fine circle of upright stones near by. It is very complete, although the stones composing it are not of great size. Near this place are many relics of exceeding interest. Kes, or Cas Tor, with its fine rock basin discovered by Mr. G. W. Ormerod and the Longstone rock pillar, with some fine stone avenues and village enclosures are all within a short distance, and will prove to the antiquary attractions which will detain him long, and well repay him in their examination.

Proceeding up the slope we made our way to the gate in the new-take wall, and descended by a rough track to an ancient clapper bridge over the North Teign, and not far from the solitary Teign Head farmhouse. Having just previously (when between Metherell and Fernworthy) killed a snake, the circumstance reminded me of having done a similar thing a few years before, close to this old bridge, and I pointed out the spot to my companion, at the same time relating to him some incidents of various rambles which I had enjoyed over this ground on previous occasions.

The bridge is a very good specimen, although not so interesting as some others on the moor. The imposts are not nearly so large as those at Post Bridge or Bellaford. There they consist of slabs of granite of immense size, while in this, though the stones are by no means small, they are of a different character, being long blocks about two feet, or rather more, in width. My measurements of this old structure, which are carefully preserved in my note-book, show it to be twenty-seven feet eight inches in length, and

M

six feet nine inches in breadth. There are two piers built
in the river, forming three openings for the stream to pass
through, and over each opening are laid three stones. The
height of the road way from the bed of the river is not very
great, only four feet eight inches, but it is sufficient to
admit of the stream flowing freely on, even when its volume
is increased by " floods," as the bridge being near the upper
waters of the Teign it is not here a stream of great size.

There is a kind of causeway leading to it on each side, of
a similar character to that to be seen approaching the
bridge at Dartmeet. It is more plainly to be seen on the
side of the river on which Teign Head farm-house is
situated, although it is not pointing immediately towards it,
its direction being north-west by north, while the house lies
due west.

Teign Head farm-house is one of the most solitary on all
Dartmoor, being far removed from any other habitation,
and adjoining some of the wildest parts of the moor. A
stranger unaware of its existence would certainly be
surprised at coming across a dwelling in such a remote spot.
Its situation on such a high part of Dartmoor, although it
is fairly well sheltered by rising ground around it, must
have exposed it to the pitiless severity of many a winter
storm ; but the old house looks none the worse for
the fury of the mountain winds which have beat against it,
its grey granite walls seeming to bid defiance to the attacks
of the elements.

Leaving the farm-house at some distance on our left hand,
we mounted the slope which rises from the river, and made
our way across the new-take to White Horse Hill, an
eminence from whence a goodly view of the surrounding

moor is to be obtained. From here we passed onward to East Dart Head, where we called a halt, and rested for awhile at my Chair. The day was a very hot one, and we were not sorry to repose for a short time among the heather. After having refreshed ourselves we arose and struck out over the bogs for Cranmere Pool, which, as I have already observed, is but a very short distance from the springs of the East Dart.

To call it a pool seems now somewhat of a misnomer, for unfortunately it is not at present capable of containing any quantity of water, the northern bank having been broken through. When this was done I know not ; Mr. Rowe, in his *Perambulation of Dartmoor*, speaks of it as being in that state in July 1844, but it would not appear to have been so when it was first visited by the Rev. E. A. Bray, in September 1802,* although it is, of course, possible that he may not have sufficiently examined the bank to observe this. At all events, in referring to the capacity of the pool, he remarks that the water could not be more than six or eight feet deep when it was full. It was dry when he saw it, and through it he observed the footmarks of a fox, and also walked into it some little distance, but it is clear from his statement of the pool being capable of holding water to the depth of six or eight feet, either that the bank was then not broken, or that he did not observe it, or (which is by no means improbable) that the opening was not then of the same proportions as it is now.

I have heard two explanations given of the bank being broken : one, that during a summer drought it was cut

---

* *Vide* extracts from his journal in Mrs. Bray's *Borders of the Tamar and the Tavy*, Vol. I. p. 261. First ed.

through in order to empty the waters of the pool into the
West Ockment, which rises very near to it, by a miller living
near Okehampton, whose mill was driven by that stream; the
other, that sheep having sometimes fallen into it and been
drowned, the danger was removed by draining the pool.   I
consider the first the most likely reason of Cranmere being
emptied of its waters.

At present a great portion of the bottom of the pool is
overgrown with heather.   During summer the only water
seen in it is contained in little ponds on the peat; in winter,
there is, of course, much more, but as I have explained, it
is not capable now of holding it in any quantity.   That its
bank should have been thus broken, and Cranmere transformed from a mountain tarn to a mere boggy hollow, and
a natural curiosity be lost to us, is much to be regretted,
and affords an instance among the many to be found on
Dartmoor of objects of interest having suffered at the hands
of the careless and the ignorant.

Mr. Rowe gives the circumference of this pool as two
hundred and twenty yards, but this measurement is
obtained by including all the broken ground on its western
side within its area.   Leaving this out, a careful measurement showed me that the pool proper is twenty-eight yards
less than this, or one hundred and ninety-two yards in
circumference.   It is situated at an elevation of over
eighteen hundred feet.

But though the pool itself may be disappointing to the
visitor who has braved the toil of journeying to it, its
surroundings certainly cannot be.   Dreary, in one sense,
they may be, but they yet influence and attract, for here we
behold nature in her most wild form.   Long stretches of

moorland sweep out on every side, covered with the coarse grass that grows on the peat bogs, and scarcely a trace of man's hand is to be observed. A lonely, desolate spot, forsaken even by the cattle and wild ponies of the forest, but yet affording a far off glimpse of the cultivated world beyond those hills which form a barrier to the north. For to the left of Yes Tor, which is in full view from the pool, one looks down the valley of the West Ockment, and in the distance sees through the narrow opening, the smiling fields, —a small patch of cultivation, it is true, but yet serving to show more fully the utter barrenness of the deserted moor.

But many spots around the pool are of a wilder and more desolate nature than Cranmere itself, for there the view towards the north, embracing Ockment Hill on one side, with Amicombe Hill on the other, and the range of High Wilhayes, Yes Tor, West Mil Tor and Row Tor, and the glimpse of cultivation just referred to, while it undoubtedly adds to the interest, serves somewhat to lessen the desolateness of the scene. By the upper waters of the Dart, described in Chapter VII, which are immediately in this district, and where the ground possesses precisely the same characteristics of a boggy, swampy nature, there are many spots far more desolate, because of their surroundings being more contracted, and permitting of no view of the outer world.

And it is to these spots the visitor to Cranmere ought to go. He should not look upon the pool itself as the goal of his pilgrimage to this remote region, but would do well to bestow upon the district around some share of his attention. Of course the ordinary visitor to Cranmere will not have time to see much of this, for he would find it would take him many days to explore in anything approaching a complete manner the wild surroundings, but he may gain an idea of what they are like by going over a portion of the ground between the pool and Tavy Head, or in the direction of Cut Hill, or by the side of the Dart.

In the pool is a little heap of stones, and in a hollow in this is kept a small tin box,—I have seen two there—for the reception of the cards of visitors. The spirit of vandalism, unfortunately but too prevalent, may have intruded itself here, but, on the whole, the contents of the boxes seem to be respected. I can at all events affirm that I have found names there—my own among others—which had been left at the pool several years before.

The pool is traditionally said to be haunted by the spirit of Benjamin Gayer, (familiarly called Bingie Gear) erewhile mayor of the good borough of Okehampton. For what cause his shade was condemned to wander by its dark water, the gossips know not. They aver, however, that one of the punishments inflicted upon the unhappy Bingie, was that of being doomed to dip out the pool—not with a limpet shell with a hole in it—but with a sieve. At this hopeless task it seems he spent his time, until, by good fortune, he found one day upon the moor, the carcase of a sheep, and taking the skin covered the seive with it, and setting hastily to work, soon emptied the pool. The increase of water in the Ockment was so great, that it rolled down from the hills in a mighty flood, and drowned the town over which he had presided as mayor in his " days of nature."

Whether this legend suggested to the miller who is said to have dug through the bank, a means of increasing the supply of water to his mill, or whether (which is more

likely) the act of the miller gave rise to the story, is a point
I cannot, of course, determine, but that the pool is now
comparatively empty I can most certainly aver.

Another tradition states that Bingie is condemned to
haunt the pool in the form of a black colt. I would not,
however, advise the visitor who may encounter such an
animal near the bogs of Cranmere, to too hastily conclude
that he beholds the restless spirit of Okehampton's departed
mayor, for although the place is shunned by the Dartmoor
ponies that range the wild hills of the north quarter, yet it
is, of course, no unlikely circumstance that occasionlly one
may wander near it, and perchance, too, of a sable hue.

In Okehampton the following charm is said to be effectual
in raising the spirit of the unhappy Bengie. If it is not
found so, the failure must be attributed to want of faith on
the part of the person performing the incantation, or to the
fact of Bengie not being within hearing. It is exceedingly
simple, and does not require any midnight visits to the
churchyard, or circle of skulls à la Der Freischutz, the
person desirous of summoning the spirit merely observing
the following brief instructions. He must walk three times
around the table (the gentle reader will perceive that this
charm is supposed to be worked in a room : it is not adapted
for raising the spirit on its native heath) *from east to west,*
repeating at the same time these words :

> " Bingie Gear, Bingie Gear,
> If thou art near
> Do thou appear ! "

The young lady from whom I learnt this valuable charm,
told me at the same time of an old man, resident in
Okehampton, who placed the most implicit confidence in its

power, and could never be got to repeat it, *when walking around the table.* However, by dint of a great amount of coaxing he was at length induced to go through the ceremony for the benefit of my informant and her friends. Strange to say, there was no result,—that is, not *immediately.* But that very night a terrible thunder storm burst over the town, and the old man verily believed that Bingie had come to visit him! The next morning, although he found himself safe and sound, he was so terrified at what had occurred that he declared that he would never work the charm again whatever inducement might be offered him.

It was formerly supposed that Cranmere Pool was the source of several of the Dartmoor rivers, while in reality it is the source of none. Since the bank has been cut through water can no longer accumulate in it to any depth, but as such drains from the surrounding bogs into it, from which source the pool obtains its supply, it runs off through the artificial channel into the springs of the West Ockment, and in this manner a connection does exist between it and that river. But it is not a natural one, and the springs of the Ockment are entirely independent of the pool, although rising nearer to it than any other stream. The East Dart, the Taw, and the Tavy have also their sources very near it, and these four streams are really the whole that rise from the Cranmere bogs. The north Teign is generally said to do so, but between the boggy land where rise the four streams mentioned and the source of the latter river, there is a high ridge of harder ground, and it is also at some distance off, so it cannot therefore be truly said to take its rise from the morasses of Cranmere.

When we once more reached the Dart at a short distance

below its springs, just as the afternoon was drawing to its close, we neither of us felt averse to resting awhile, for our ramblings had extended over the bogs towards Great Kneeset and Tavy Head.   Seeking a convenient spot, which has more than once been my halting place,—where stand the scanty vestiges of a little mining hut by a small tributary rivulet,—we sat down and made a further onslaught upon our wallets.   By the time we resumed our journey the sun was sinking, and long shadows lay upon the heath.   Instead of pursuing our way down by the Dart, which, however, affords by far the best path, there being good hard ground close to its banks, I struck out over the boggy ground between that river and White Horse Hill, reaching the stream again at a short distance above the pass at Sandy Hole, described in Chapter VII.

Down through the pass we went, which in the fast approaching twilight looked cold and gloomy, and emerging at the bottom, made away across the darkening moor in the direction of Row Tor Gate.   Gaining the new-take we pushed on, passing near Arch Tor, and so descended to the Princetown and Moreton Road, reaching it just as darkness fell on all around.   As we passed on by the new-take walls under Bellaford Tor, we could look across the few miles of moor that intervened between us and Princetown and see the lighted windows of the prisons, all the rest of the moor being shrouded in darkness.

Passing Dunnabridge Pound we reached the Ashburton road, along which we made our way towards Hexworthy, for I had determined upon stopping there for the night. As we turned down the road opposite Brimpts plantation we heard a footstep, and halting to see whom it might be, I found it was old George Caunter of Dartmeet—Uncle George, as we call him—returning home. A brief stoppage to exchange a few words with the old man—it was too late to "stop tellin'" very long—and on we went again, reaching soon after the hospitable shelter of the Forest Inn.

It was about half-past ten, and all the inmates but the good landlady, Mrs. Cleave, had retired to rest. However, the fire on the hearth was quickly coaxed into a blaze, and we were soon made comfortable in the cozy kitchen. Mrs. Cleave was rather perplexed about the sleeping arrangements, not having expected me, and the room which was always assigned to me being occupied by a passing angler, who had sought shelter for the night. But this was got over by my companion getting into bed with one of the sons, (which he so stealthily effected that he did not awake him, and even left him still sleeping when he rose in the morning) while with the aid of blankets and sheets I was made comfortable on the sofa in the little parlour.

I will not relate how in the morning we strolled around the little hamlet, chatting with one and another of the dwellers there, or how in the bright forenoon we set out across the hills on our way to Brent, for having conducted the reader to Cranmere, and also brought him safely away from its desolate swamps. I will, while the dark shades of night are resting on the moor, and silence is reigning over that lonely region, bid him farewell; and if the perusal of this account of some few of my wanderings on Dartmoor shall have been the means of affording him but a small portion of the pleasure that the rambles have given me, I shall venture to believe that he does not regret having for a little space lent me his attention.

APPENDIX.

APPENDIX.

LIST OF THE TORS AND PRINCIPAL HILLS OF DARTMOOR.

THOSE piles of granite rocks, known as tors, crowning so many of the eminences of Dartmoor, and assuming strange and fantastic shapes, lend to the district a great deal of its wildness, and constitute one of its principal attractions.

The word *tor*, which is of Celtic origin, and found in slightly varying forms in Cornish, Welsh and Gaelic,* seems to imply altitude, being almost synonymous with the word *tower*.

What I consider an amusing instance of confusing this latter word with that of *tor*, occurs in the notes to Cottle's poem on *Dartmoor*.† After speaking of the round towers of Ireland, the writer says " Several towers, somewhat similar to these, are now to be seen on Dartmoor, but for what purpose they were erected, or at what period, far removed, as they must have been, is unknown—see

---

* Rowe in his *Perambulation of Dartmoor*, p. 7, ed. 1848, gives Cornish *tor*, Welsh *twr*, and Irish Gaelic *tor*; and in Murray's Hand-book for Devon, p. 195, ed. 1879, the word is said to be apparently cognate with the Hebrew *tsoor*, a rock, and the Phœnician *tor*, Tyre.

† *Dartmoor, and other Poems*, by Joseph Cottle, 1823.

Archæologia, vol. I." Now, as no towers of any kind exist on Dartmoor, either like the Irish round towers or any others, I can only imagine that the writer of the note—who could have had no real acquaintance with the moor—confused the word *tor* with *tower*, and their reputed similarity to the Irish towers must have been a creation of his fancy, or of somebody else's whom he followed.

With the exception of some few of the most insignificant the tors of Dartmoor possess names, and of the derivation of these a great deal might be written, though as yet not much has been done in this direction. Mr. R. N. Worth in a paper in the tenth volume of the *Transactions of the Devonshire Association* (1878) * has given us some valuable information on this subject, and Mr. Spence Bate has also done good work in this direction, though not so much in connection with the tors as with the streams of the moor, in a paper in the fourth volume of the *Transactions* of the same Association (1871),† and other writers have touched upon it, but nothing approaching an exhaustive treatise on the subject has yet appeared. To enter upon an examination of the names of these tors, would prove a great task—to break ground upon the subject, even, would be no mean one—and it is not my design to venture upon this now, but I cannot let the subject pass without saying a word or two in order to caution the reader against too readily accepting some of the explanations which have been offered of these names.§

---

* *Notes on the Historical Connections of Devonshire Place-Names.*

† *A Contribution towards Determining the Etymology of Dartmoor Names.*

§ I do not allude to explanations given in either of the papers I have just referred to.

Several of the tors bear the names of familiar objects and animals, and credence has too readily been given to the idea that this has arisen from their possessing a resemblance to such. That a few have received their appellations from such a cause I am not disposed to doubt ; such, for instance, as Bench Tor and Kes or Kest Tor, (this latter presenting a rude resemblance to a huge *kist*, or chest)* but that the familiar examples which are generally adduced in support of this view owe their names to any such source, to those who have a real acquaintance with the tors of Dartmoor, must appear absurd. Take such an instance as Hare Tor. Can anyone who knows it pretend to say that its outline, from whichever side it may be viewed, presents any resemblance to the form of that animal ? The Rev. E. A. Bray † speaks of this tor as Hare or Air Tor. We venture to think that even if the " animal likeness " theory be abandoned by the credulous etymologist who *must* give the sounds of ancient words a modern meaning, he will scarcely fall back on the second of these names, but will rather be inclined to suffer his speculations to melt into the element itself. Again : would Hound Tor ever remind the beholder of a dog, or Fox Tor call forth thoughts of Reynard ? Or would Hen Tor arouse the enthusiasm of a poultry fancier ? Yet those who believe in this kind of thing must consider the resemblances to be exceedingly striking, for not only, it seems, is the form of the particular animal or bird to be clearly seen but even its very sex may be distinguished. For here, they say, we have Fox Tor, and yonder is Vixen

---

* Murray. p. 131. ed. 1879.

† *Tamar and the Tavy* Vol. I. p. 277. first ed.

Tor; here is Hare Tor, yonder is Doe Tor; here is Cocks Tor, yonder is Hen Tor!

That these names are corruptions of the original ones, the meanings of which are forgotten, there is, I think, little room to doubt * We see this exemplified in the case of Sheep's Tor, which is one of those which the race of "animal likeness" etymologists have pounced upon, † though rather unfortunately for their theory. The ancient name was not Sheep's Tor, but Schitestor or Shettistore, showing plainly that the modern appellation is in no way referable to the ovine species, but is simply a corruption of the old name. Those, however, who cannot dissociate the animal in question from the tor, and in spite of un-impeachable documentary evidence to the contrary will *revenons à leurs moutons*, may content themselves with the knowledge that sheep in plenty roam around it, and thus it is consequently a *sheep's* tor, after all !

But these etymologists aim at something more romantic when they seek to derive the names of certain of the tors from those of heathen deities, and exalt the rocks of Dartmoor into Druid altars. The reader may see some of these examples in Mrs. Bray's *Tamar and Tavy*, Vol. I. p. 57, where she has followed Borlase and Polwhele. Ham (or Hameldon) Tor is there derived from the heathen god Ammon ; Hessary from Hesus, or Esus (this is very rich ; there is really no such tor,—its proper name being Hisworthy, and is so spelt in the perambulations, but now

---

* See a paper on *Dartmoor and the Walkham* by Frederick Pollock, in the *English Illustrated Magazine* for January 1884.

† In the notes to Carrington's *Dartmoor* (1826) the names of nine tors are given to which it is sought to attach such a derivation.

corrupted in the Devonshire vernacular to Hessary) ; Mis
Tor from Misor or Miser.* and Bel Tor from Bel, or Baal!
That Bel Tor, Belstone, Bellaford, Bala Brook, etc. are in
close proximity to ancient mine workings—or bals—these
enthusiastic word-hunters take no account, but being
infected so deeply with Druidophobia, can receive no
explanation unless it be connected with heathen gods and
altars. In Chapter VIII. I have referred to the probable
derivation of the name of the Dewerstone. To most people
I should imagine such would commend itself. But not so
to those that suffer from this mania of importing heathen
divinities into Dartmoor, for *Dwr* does not satisfy them,
and so they suggest *Tiw*, the name of a deity worshipped
by the Saxons.

As Mrs Bray followed Borlase and Polwhele, so many in
their turn have followed her, but a candid examination
made without a " Druid bias " must result in the rejection
of any such far-fetched and improbable derivations of these
names.

Mr. R. J. King, who possessed an intimate knowledge of
the moor, has helped us to the meanings of several of the
names of the tors, as also has Mr. R. N. Worth in the
paper to which I have already referred. The former
writer in his work entitled *The Forest of Dartmoor, and its
Borders,* (1856) has given us Roose Tor, the red or heathery
hill, from the Cornu *rooz, red ;* Mil Tor, the yellow hill,
from *mel, yellow ;* Links Tor, the hill of the marsh, from
lynnek, lynnick, wet, marshy ; Kneeset, the great mossy hill,
from *neage, moss,* and Crockern Tor, from *chrecken, or*

---

* See remarks as to this in Chap. V. *ante*

N

chrocken, which signifies *a little hill*.   Mr. Worth has given
us among others Hameldon, which he says *may* be *ymyl-don*,
the *boundary hill*; Dunnagoat *dun-y-coed*, the *wooded hill*,
which is British; Lough Tor, perhaps "low tor"; Mis
(mist) Tor; Pu or Pew Tor, which he suggests may be
from the same root as "pew" in a church, in consequence
of the singular rock enclosure of its summit (*pew*=literally,
a raised place); Rippon Tor, from *rypan*, to *tear up*;
Sittaford, or Siddaford Tor, from *sith* a *path*, and Yes Tor
from *yst*, *storm*, all of Saxon derivation.   Lether Tor he
derives from the Saxon *hlith*, a *declivity*, or *slope*, and not
from the Cornu, *ledr*, a *cliff*.   Mr. Worth also refers to
Crockern Tor, mentioning as possible derivations, the Saxon
croc, a *barrow*, and *ern*, a *place*, or an *eagle*, as well as the
Cornu *carreg*, a *rock*.

The reader will also find the names of several of the
Dartmoor tors explained in Murray's *Handbook for Devon*,
among which may be mentioned Fur Tor, from the Saxon
feor, *far*; Hey Tor, from *heah*, *high*, also a Saxon word;
Brent Tor, from *brennan*, *to burn*; Kes Tor, probably from
kist, a *chest*; Thurlstone, an opening between the rocks of
Watern Tor, from *thyrelan*, to *pierce*, and Hel Tor, which
name, it is there suggested, is also found in Helvellyn, and
indicates height; this is Celtic.   High Wilhayes it is also
considered is derivable either from the Cornu *huel*, a *mine*,
or from the *wealhas*, the name given to the ancient Britons.

The old names of not a few of the Dartmoor tors are
entirely forgotten (supposing them all, at one time, to have
possessed such,) and these now bear modern appellations
setting forth their peculiarities.   Sharp Tor is a familiar
example, those bearing that name being for the most part

conical peaks; Rough Tor, Black Tor, Grey Tor, Bench Tor,* are others.

The moor-men have a habit of indulging in a reduplication of the final syllable of the names of the tors, and owing to this, and also to their pronunciation, the appellations of many have been distorted. Thus Lough Tor is changed to Loughter or Laughter Tor, Hen Tor to Henter Tor, Har Tor to Harter Tor, Inga (sometimes erroneously given as Inky) Tor to Ingater Tor—or rather, as the moor-men render it—Innater *Tar* (with them *tor* is almost invariably pronounced *tar*,) and Sharp Tor we find changed by them into Sharpy Tor.

Another habit of theirs is to add the word *rocks* to the name sometimes; thus we have Hey Tor Rocks, Hounter (Hound Tor) Rocks, etc. Indifference on the part of some writers to the correct forms of spelling, and the old ordnance map, as well as other local ones, have been fruitful sources of the erroneous orthography of many of the tors. Thus a small pile of rocks, sometimes known as Sharp Tor, near Widecombe, is named on some maps Charbe Tor; Corndon Tor is given as Quarnian Tor; Three Barrows (which is a hill on which are three large caiars, and not a tor at all) is set down as Three Barrow Tor; Petre's Cross (the name of an old cross on Western Whitaburrow, a high hill) is given as Peter's Cross Tor, while there is really no tor anywhere near it;—indeed numerous other instances might be given where such errors occur.

* Called by the moor-men Benchy or Benjy Tor.

The tors of Dartmoor, which now rise in such grand and noble proportions, delighting the lover of wild nature with their rugged forms, probably owe their origin to volcanic influences. This character of Dartmoor is considered by Mr. R. N. Worth[*] as a necessity required to account for its present condition, and is also to be proved, he maintains, by its constitution, and from the existence of rocks around its borders of an eruptive character. Dartmoor was, Mr. Worth submits, as far back as the secondary and tertiary periods, the basis of volcanic action. His theory is that the moor was originally one mountain, which, as he affirms, there are indications to lead us to suppose assumed the form of a ridge with a double peak, and the most probable of the calculations he has made as to its height show it to have been about 18,000 feet. This is a great height, certainly, but the granite, being, as we know, the primary rock, the various strata lying upon it would require it to be nothing less. On the cessation of the volcanic action denudation commenced, and gradually the mountain through millions of years has, from its height of 18,000 feet, owing to this wearing away of the super-incumbent strata, diminished to the height we see it now, and the granite has become exposed.

That ice was an important factor in the process of denudation is more than probable, and that it also has been so in the disposition of the granite blocks that are now scattered over the moor, there can be no doubt. Around the tors, and on the slopes of the hills, are not infrequently seen confused masses of boulders, covering the ground sometimes for a considerable distance, and known

[*] In a paper read before the members of the *Plymouth Institution*, (1888).

as clatters, or clitters. These masses are heaped together in the utmost confusion, suggesting to the beholder the battle ground of angry giants, who had been engaged in hurling rocks at each other in furious rage. These rocks, it is most probable, were rent from the tors by the action of frost, and slid down the ice-covered sides of the hills to their present positions, in ages long past, when the conditions of climate were different from those now existing on the moor. The clatters, which often occupy large areas of ground, give a wild and rugged appearance to the slopes of the moor.

The proportions of many of the tors are remarkably grand; the huge masses of rock being piled up in a marvellous manner, and frequently assuming the most strange forms. Often do they stand as if placed by some wizard hand to guard the pass below, and grim and dark they lift their heads above the brown heath around. By far the greater number are situated on the moors surrounding the forest, and not within the bounds of the forest itself, and the finest are those on the north, the north-west, and the south-east portions of the moor. The south quarter of the forest, and the commons adjoining it are somewhat deficient in tors, but while this is so that portion of Dartmoor is not the less interesting, for it possesses some of the finest prehistoric monuments to be found upon it, so that man by his works in the past has left that which creates an interest for us to-day, and consoles us for the loss of what nature has withheld. In the south quarter of the forest itself, Fox Tor, and one small un-named tor, are all that are to be found, and on the nine commons which border upon that quarter (I reckon Walkhampton Common as abutting upon the west quarter) only about a score are situated.

Some of the tors cover large areas. Sheeps Tor is said to occupy one hundred acres; * Great Mis Tor stands on a very large space of ground,—so does Hound Tor. Many of them, too, are of great height above the hill on which they are situated, the last named rising, according to the opinion of Mr. Rowe,† though I cannot say I have ever verified it, to eighty or one hundred feet above the ground.

There is some small difficulty in compiling a list of the tors of Dartmoor, on account of deciding what really are or are not such, several of the hills which have been some-times reckoned as tors, possessing no crown of granite rocks to entitle them to that designation. The only list which has yet been formed is to be found in the Notes to Carrington's poem of *Dartmoor*, which includes those named by Colonel Mudge on the ordance survey map, published in 1809, but it is very far from being correct, and the hills and tors are all mixed up together. For instance, such names are given as being those of tors as Knattleborough, Huntingdon, Avon, or Aune Head, and Eastern Whita-burrow. Now no such tors as these exist. The first and second are hills with a cairn on each of them, Aune Head has no tor anywhere nearer to it than Fox Tor, and that is about a mile distant, and Eastern Whitaburrow is a large cairn crowning a hill on Brent Moor. Many other instances of similar mistakes might be given.

---

* Notes to Carrington's *Dartmoor*, p. 177. A French writer, M. Jules Poulain, in an interesting story, entitled *Le Dartmoor, ou Les Deux Sœurs*, published in Paris in 1852, refers to the size of this tor.

† *Perambulation of Dartmoor* p. 123. first ed.

In the following list I have been careful to include only such as are in reality tors, *i.e.*, piles of rock, and have placed the hills on which tors do not exist in a separate catalogue. I have given all the tors of the moor, but in the list of hills only the principal are named. To mention all these would be to lengthen the list unnecessarily, as will be seen when I inform the reader that almost every eminence, or swelling on the moor, however small it may be, possesses a name. There are a few tors in the neighbourhood of Chagford, Lustleigh and Bovey; these are not included among the others, as they certainly cannot be said to be on Dartmoor now, the commons on which they stand being separated from it by cultivated country, so I have given their names in a separate list. Brent Tor and Brent Hill are also named separately, as although near the moor, they are not actually upon it. The heights of the more important tors and hills are given in feet; these are according to the recent Ordnance Survey and are for the most part surface elevations.

LIST OF THE TORS, ETC.

The names of the tors are arranged in five groups: one for each of the quarters of the forest and the commons abutting on them, and one for that portion of the moor which lies to the eastward of the Widecombe Valley, and in each group the names are given in alphabetical order.

I.

The North Quarter and Commons bordering upon it.

Arms Tor, near Lydford.

Ashbury Tor, Okehampton Park. Near this is Belstone Cleave, a romantic glen.

Belstone Tor, 1537, near Belstone Village.

Black Tor, 1646, West Ockment. Below this is Black Tor Copse, an ancient oak wood; and the Island of Rocks, an enchanting spot, where are some fine cascades.

Bra, or Broad Tor, 1510, near Lydford.

Chat Tor, 1774, on Rattle Brook, Tavy.

Dinger Tor, 1810, near Yes Tor.

Doe Tor, near Lydford.

Dunnagoat Tor (Higher), 1845, Rattle Brook, Tavy.

Dunnagoat Tor (Lower), 1832,   do.   do.

Fur Tor, 1877, at Tavy Head. This tor is in a wild and desolate district.

Gidleigh Tor, in Gidleigh Park. Generally known in the neighbourhood as Princep's Folly; on it are the ruins of a house built about forty years since by a Mr. Princep, and which was soon deserted.

Green Tor, 1774, near Rattle Brook, Tavy.

Gren Tor, 1693, at head of Lyd.

Higber Tor, one of the Belstone group.

Hound Tor, 1622, near Steeperton Tor. Called in the perambulation of 1609 *Little* Hound Tor.

Hunt Tor, 1843, Rattle Brook Head, Tavy.

Ivy Tor, on bank of Taw above Sticklepath.

Kit, or Kitty Tor, 1920, near Stinka Tor.

Links Tor (Great), 1908, near Rattle Brook Head, Tavy.
Links Tor (Little), 1677   do.   do.
Lints Tor, 1605, near Dinger Tor.

Mil Tor (East), 1683, south of Okehampton Park, near Yes Tor.
Mil Tor (West),   do.   do.   do.

Ock, or Oke Tor, to the south of the Belstone group.

Rival Tor, on tributary of the Wallabrook, North Teign ; a small tor on a grassy hill.

Row, or Rough Tor, near East and West Mil Tors.

Scarey Tor, on East Ockment, below the Belstone group.

Scorhill Tor, on the hillside below confluence of North Teign and Wallabrook, more often called Scorhill Rocks.   In close proximity to this tor are many objects of interest—notably, the celebrated Gidleigh stone circle, the largest of the kind on the Moor ; the tolmen, or holed stone, in the bed of the Teign ; and a single stone clapper bridge over the Wallabrook. These are described by Mr. Rowe (*Perambulation*) and by Mr. G. W. Ormerod (*Archæological Memoirs*).

Sharp Tor, 1701, on Rattle Brook, Tavy.

Shilstone Tor, near Throwleigh.

Shilstone Tor, near Sourton.

Sourton Tors, a group of several above Sourton Village.

Steeperton Tor, 1738, upper portion of Taw, southward of Ock Tor.

Stinka, or Steinga Tor, on the hill to west of Sandy Ford, West Ockment.

Watern, or Waterdon Tor, 1756, Wallabrook, Teign. A portion of this tor is known as Thurlstone, where there is a curious opening between the rocks.

Wild Tor, 1741, near Watern Tor.
Winter Tor, the southernmost of the Belstone group.

Yes Tor, 2027, neighbourhood of Okehampton.

[On some maps will be seen marked Litorally Tor, between the North Teign and the Wallabrook, at a short distance above the

point of confluence. No such tor exists. On the rising ground
there a small clatter, or clitter, may be seen, and I suspect that
this word has somehow been transformed into Litorally, and
applied to a supposed tor. In this immediate neighbourhood
there seems to be a tendency to call hills on which are no rock
piles, tors ; for a small hill not far off is sometimes spoken of as
Round Tor, and in the vicinity we have also Stonetor Hill.]

II.
The East Quarter and Commons, etc.

Arch Tor, between Archerton, near Post Bridge, and Powder Mills.

Bel Tor, near Pound's Gate, a small but interesting tor, with numerous
rock-basins upon it.

Bellaford Tor, between Post Bridge and Dunnabridge Pound.

Birch Tor, neighbourhood of Warren House Inn.

Blackadon Tor, near Leusdon, on the borders of the moor.

Corndon Tor, above the village of Ponsworthy. There are large cairns
on this hill.

Crockern Tor, neighbourhood of Two Bridges, celebrated as the spot
on which, in old times, the stannary parliaments were held (page
84). It is probable that these meetings of the tinners date back
to the 13th century, though the first of which we have any account
was not held till the end of the 15th (1494).

Frenchbeer Tor, near Kes Tor.

Hameldon Tor, at north end of Hameldon.

Hartland Tor, 1351, on East Dart above Post Bridge.

Hockinston Tor, below Mil Tor, on Dart.

Hookney Tor, Shapeley Common.

Huccaby Tor, between Brimpts and Dunnabridge Pound.

King Tor, Shapeley Common.

Kes, or Cas Tor, 1433, neighbourhood of Chagford. On this tor is a very
large rock-basin discovered by Mr. Ormerod, and on the common
near by a fine series of pre-historic remains. These consist of stone
avenues (page 37), a portion of a cromlech, or dolmen, known as
the "Three Boys," and a fine upright granite pillar—the Longstone ; numerous hut circles in a fine state of preservation, the
Round Pound, &c. This group of antiquities has been fully described by Mr. Ormerod, who has also given a plan of them. A
plan has also been made by Sir Gardner Wilkinson.

Leigh Tor, Pound's Gate.

Littaford Tors, a small group near Longaford Tor, marked on some
maps as Little Bee Tor, &c.

Longaford Tor, 1595, eastward of West Dart, above Wistman's Wood.

Lough, or Laugh Tor, between East Dart and Huccaby Tor.

Loughten Tor. This is not called a tor by the moor people. It is a small pile of rocks in the new-take on Loughten Hill, opposite Fernworthy.

Lug Tor, on Dart, under Rowbrook Farm, below Dartmeet.

Middle Tor, near Kes Tor.

Mil Tor, on Dart, below Dartmeet.

Row, or Rough Tor, 1791, on West Dart, north of Wistman's Wood.

Siddaford Tor, 1764, neighbourhood of Teign Head.

Shapeley Tor, Shapeley Common.

Sharp Tor, on Dart, below Dartmeet.

Stannon, or Standon Tor, behind Standon House, (now labourer's cottage), neighbourhood of Post Bridge.

Thornworthy Tor, near Thornworthy Farm, not far from South Teign.

White Tor (Higher), near Longaford Tor.

White Tor (Lower), 　　　do. 　　　do.

Wind Tor, Dunstone Down, near Widecombe Village.

Yar Tor, on East Dart, just above Dartmeet.
　[A small pile on the common near Pound's Gate is sometimes known as Aish Tor.]

III.

The Commons to the Eastward of the Widecombe Valley.

Bag Tor, Bag Tor Down, Ilsington.

Bel Tor, above Widecombe Village.

Bonehill Rocks 　　　ditto 　　　do.

Buckland Beacon, near Buckland-in-the-Moor, neighbourhood of Ashburton.

Chinkwell Tor, 1504, near Bonehill Rocks.

East Down Tor, 1438, near Manaton.

Grea, or Grey Tor, near Hound Tor, Manaton.

Hey Tor, 1491, neighbourhood of Ilsington, a well-known tor, consisting of two fine castellated piles of rock.

Hollow Tor, near Rugglestone, Widecombe village.

Holwill Tor, near Hey Tor.

Honeybag Tor, near head of Widecombe valley. A very fine tor.
Hound Tor, near Manaton. Very high rocks ; a grand pile.

Manaton Tor, above Manaton village, often called Manaton Rocks.

Pil Tor, near Hollow Tor.

Rippon Tor, 1563, near Ilsington. Near the summit is a fine logan stone known as the " Nutcracker."

Saddle Tor, between Rippon Tor and Hey Tor.
Sharp Tor, small tor near Widecombe Village.*

Top Tor or Torhill, near Widecombe Village.

IV

The South Quarter and Commons, etc.

Beacon Rocks, 1230. Eastern Beacon, Ugborough Moor.
Bench Tor, above the Dart Valley, on Holne Moor.

Black Tor, on Avon, Brent Moor.
Black Alder Tor, near Lee Moor Clay Works.

Calveslake Tor, near head of Plym.
Collard Tor, Shaugh Moor.
Cumsdon Tor, above the Dart Valley, on Holne Moor.

Fox Tor, near head of Swincombe River, celebrated as the tor near which tradition says that Childe the Hunter, perished.

Hall Tor, or Tristis Rock, near Harford Bridge.
Hawks' Tor, Shaugh Moor.
Hen Tor, Plym, above Cadaford Bridge.

Pupers, near Hayford : Dean Moor.
　　(There are three piles here—known as Inner Pupers, Pupers Rock, 1523, and Outer Pupers.)
Sharp Tor, Erme, above Piles.
Sharp Tor, Brent Moor, between Three Barrows and Fore Hill.
Shavercombe Tor, on Shavercombe Brook, Plym.
Shipley Tor, Avon, Brent Moor.

Trowlsworthy Tor, (Great), 1141, near Cadaford Bridge, Plym.
Trowlsworthy Tor, (Little), 1062,　　　do.　　　do.
　　[On the slope near these tors are some rather curious enclosures, which have been described by Mr. Spence Bate.]

---

* On page 24 it is stated that there are five tors by this name on the moor. It should have been six. There are five on the commons which abut on the forest, and this one to the eastward of Widecombe makes a sixth. Besides these there are two Sharp Tors, as will be seen from the list, off the moor.

White Hill Tor, near Lee Moor Clay Works, sometimes called Torry Combe Tor.

[Some scattered rocks on the hill behind Rook Farm, near Cornwood, under Pen Beacon, are sometimes called Rook Tor; and on Crownhill Down, near the Lee Moor Clay Works, is a small pile occasionally known as Crownhill Tor.]

V.

The West Quarter and Commons, etc.

Bagga Tor 1219, near Standon Hill, on tributary of Tavy.

Bairdown Tor, 1679, west of West Dart, above Bairdown Farm, neighbourhood of Two Bridges.

Black Tor, Walkhampton Common, near Princetown,

Boulters Tor, Smeardon Down.

Cocks Tor, 1449, neighbourhood of Tavistock.

Combe, or Combeshead Tor, Narrator Brook, near Sheeps Tor.

Combe Tor (Great), Peter Tavy Brook.

Combe Tor (Little), do. do.

Conies' Down Tor, Conies' Down, near head of Cowsic.

Cramber Tor, Walkhampton Common, near Princetown.

Crip Tor do. do.

Crow Tor, 1646, near Bairdown Tor.

Devil's Tor, 1785 between upper waters of West Dart and Cowsic. Near it, in a wild and desolate part of the Moor, is a fine rock pillar known as Bairdown Man, nearly eleven feet high.

Down Tor, 1201, on Newleycombe Lake.

Eastern Tor, near Ditsworthy Warren house.

Feather Tor, between Merivale Bridge and Whitchurch Down.

Ger, or Great Tor, Nat Tor Down.

Gutter Tor, Ringmoor Down.

Har Tor, Walkhampton Common, near Princetown.

Har Tor (Higher), 1349, near Eylesbarrow, Plym.

Har Tor (Lower) do. do.

Hare Tor, 1744. Near this is Tavy Cleave, a wild and romantic spot.

Heckwood Tor, near Sampford Spiney.

Hisworthy Tor (North), near Princetown.

Hisworthy Tor (South), 1475, near Princetown.

Hollow Tor, near Rundle Stone Tor.

Inga Tor, close to railway, Walkhampton Common.

King Tor,   do.   do.   do.   A pile near is
     sometimes called *Little* King Tor.

Leedon Tor, near the road, Walkhampton Common. A spindle whorl
     of slate was found on this tor in 1888 by Mr. Alexander, of the
     Princetown Convict Prison.

Leggis Tor, Plym, above Cadaford Bridge.

Lether Tor, near Peek Hill, Walkhampton Common.

Lowery Tor, on Peek Hill, Walkhampton Common.

Lydford Tor, 1647, near Bairdown Tor.

Lynch Tor, near Walkham Head.

Mis Tor, (Great), 1760, Walkham. On the common near Merivale
     Bridge, in the neighbourhood of this tor, are the fine pre-historic
     monuments referred to on page 38. A plan and description of
     these were given by Mr. Rowe in 1830 ; and in Mrs. Bray's *Tamar
     and Tavy*, in 1836 Sir Gardner Wilkinson has also given us a plan,
     and one may be seen in Mr. Ferguson's work, *Rude Stone Monu-
     ments.*

Mis Tor. (Little),   do.

Nat Tor, Nat Tor Down, close to Tavy Cleave.

Pu Tor, near Sampford Spiney.

Roose, or Rolls Tor, near Mis Tor, on opposite side of the Walkham.

Rundle Stone Tor, close to Rundle Stone, Princetown.

Sharp Tor, near Lether Tor.

Sheeps Tor, above Sheepstor Village.

Staple Tor (Great), near Roose Tor.

Staple Tor (Mid.),   do.   do.

Staple Tor (Little),   do.   do.

Vixen Tor, near Merivale Bridge. Sometimes called the Sphinx Rock.

White Tor, Cudlip Town Down.

     [On Callisham Down, near Meavy, is a small tor known as Cal-
     lisham Tor, and near the Blackabrook, not far from Tor Royal,
     is a small un-named tor which seems to be the one which Mr.
     Rowe (*Trans. Plymo. Institution*, vol. I., 1830), speaks of as
     Colden Tor ; but I have never heard it so called in the neigh-
     bourhood.

     The Rev. E. A. Bray, speaks of Swell Tor, on Walkhampton
     Common. The Swell Tor granite quarry now exists on its site.
     Foggin Tor quarries were probably also formed on the site of a
     tor. Mr. Bray makes mention of Yeast Tor near here. There are
     many scattered piles on this part of the common ; one of them,
     below King Tor, is sometimes spoken of as Hucken Tor.   This

writer also speaks of Over Tor : this seems to be the one now called Little Mis Tor.

Some piles in the neighbourhood of Sheeps Tor are known as Rough Tor and Click Tor.]

Rock Piles on Dartmoor not reckoned as Tors.

Bowerman's Nose. There are two small tors near it on Hayne Down.
Branscombe's Loaf and Cheese, not far from Great Links Tor.

Dewerstone, confluence of Plym and Meavy.

Foresland Ledge, near Yes Tor.

Greator Rocks, sometimes called Leighon Tor, near Grea Tor.

Hangershell Rock, near Butterdon Hill.
Hemstone Rocks, near Fernworthy.

Slipper Stones, above the left bank of the West Ockment, opposite Black Tor Copse.

Tor Rocks, near Harford.
Tunhill Rocks, near Blackslade, Widecombe.

Whittenknowles Rocks, on the Plym.

[Ausewell Rock is a short distance off the moor, in Buckland Woods ; often called Hazel Rock, or Hazel Tor, near it are crags known as the Lover's Leap, and the Raven Rock.]

The principal Hills of the Moor.

Amicombe Hill.

Black Ridge, 1853, near Great Kneeset.
Butterdon Hill, 1203, near the Western Beacon, above Ivybridge.

Cater's Beam.
Cock's Hill, 1644.
Corn Ridge.
Cosdon Hill. Cosdon Beacon, 1799 feet.
Cut Hill, 1980.

Down Ridge.

East Down, or Easdon, Hill.

East Hill.
Eylesbarrow, 1491.

Great Nodder, 1430.
Green Hill.

Hameldon.   Hameldon Beacon, 1695 feet.
Hangingstone Hill, 1983, near head of Taw.
High Wilhayes, 2039.   This is the highest point of the moor.
Holne Ridge, 1579.

Kennon Hill, 1573.
Kneeset, (Great), 1863.
Kneeset (Little),

Long Ridge.

Meripit Hill, 1474.
Metherell Hill, 1503.

Ockment Hill, 1856.

Peek Hill.
Pen Beacon, 1407.

Quickbeam Hill.

Ryder's Hill.   Petre's Bound Stone on it is situated at a height of
    1694 feet.

Shell Top, 1546.
Smear Ridge.
Snowdon.
Stannon, or Standon, Hill.

Terhill, 1575,
Three Barrows, 1521.

Watern Oke, or Ock, 1593,
Weatherdon Hill, near Butterdon Hill.
Western Beacon, above Ivybridge.
Whitaburrow.
White Hill.
White Horse Hill.
White Ridge, sometimes called Woodridge Hill.
Woodcock Hill.

Tors and Rock Piles in the neighbourhood of Chagford, Drewsteignton, Lustleigh, and Bovey.

Blackingstone Rock.
Bot Tor.

Combe Tor.

Elsford Rock.

Hel Tor.
Hingston Rocks.
Hunts Tor.

John Cann's Rocks.

Middleton Hill.

Puggie Stone.

Sharp Tor, sometimes called Shap Tor.
Skat Tor.

On Lustleigh Cleave there are

Harton Chest ; Hunters' Tor ; Ravens' Tor. or Tower ; The Fox's Yard.

Sharp Tor.—The Nutcrackers. Near Lustleigh Cleave are Gradner Rocks.

Brent Hill, 1017, in the parish of South Brent, close to the borders of the moor.

Brent Tor, 1000, near Tavistock. On the summit of this tor is a small church dedicated to St. Michael de Rupe.

On the Tavy, between Hill Bridge and Harford Bridge, some Crags are known as

Brimhill Tor, Fox Tor, High Tor, and Longtimber Tor.

On Roborough Down is Roborough Rock, anciently called Ulster, or Ullestor, Rock.

LIST OF THE CHIEF DARTMOOR RIVERS WITH THEIR LARGER TRIBUTARIES.

CARRINGTON has styled Dartmoor the "land of streams," and Tristram Risdon, the Devonshire topographer of the seventeenth century, called it "the mother of many rivers," and such are indisputably apt titles. To these streams Devon owes its beauty and fertility, and were Dartmoor incapable of being utilized for any purposes whatever it would still be invaluable from an economic point of view as the fount of these perennial rivers. In character they are similar—all rapid in their course, and their channels filled with granite boulders, over which the water falling forms numerous charming cascades; and here and there are pools and stickles, where the angler may find good sport, for the brooks and streams abound in trout.

The principal rivers of Dartmoor are the Dart, the Teign, the Avon, the Erme, the Yealm and the Plym, which all fall into the English Channel; the Tavy which uniting with the Tamar above Saltash also pours its flood into the Channel; and the Taw which flows northward into the Bristol Channel at Barnstaple Bay.* All the rest of the

---

* "Witness their divers courses; some of which disburthen themselves into the British ocean; others, by long wandering, seek the Severn sea."
—RISDON'S *Survey of Devon.*

streams which rise on the moor (with the exception of the Lyd and its tributaries, which falls into the Tamar) empty their waters into one or other of these main rivers. In the following list, however, such of these streams as do not fall into others until *after* having left the moor are not classed as tributaries, though in all cases the name of the river with which they subsequently mingle their waters is given. The list commences with the Dart, and the streams as they would be met with in a course around the moor are then enumerated, their tributaries being set opposite to them. I considered this a more convenient plan than taking them alphabetically.

It is perhaps scarcely necessary to mention that there are numberless small brooks on the moor which do not possess any names at all.

RIVERS, TRIBUTARIES, SUB-TRIBUTARIES.

DART :—East Dart—Standon Brook.
       Wallabrook, or Wellabrook.

  West Dart—Cowsic.
       Blackabrook.
       Cherry Brook.
       Dunnabridge Water.
       Swincombe River.
       Cock Lake.
       Wobrook.
  The united stream receives the Wennaford Brook.

  HOLY BROOK.
  MARDLE, or MARL.
  DEAN BURN.
  HARBOURN.—All falling into the Dart off the moor.

AVON : —FISH LAKE.
         HENG LAKE.
         BUCKLAND FORD WATER.
         WEST WALLABROOK, or WELLABROOK.
         BROCKHILL STREAM.
         SMALL BROOK.
         RED BROOK.—Middle Brook.
               Bala Brook.

      GLAZE :—EAST GLAZE.
             WEST GLAZE.

The united stream receives the Scud, and falls into the Avon off the moor.

      LUD BROOK—Falls into the Erme off the moor.

ERME :—DARK LAKE, from Black Lane.
         HOPTONSFORD BROOK.
         DRY LAKE, from Middle Mires.
         RED LAKE.
         HOOK LAKE.
         DRY LAKE, from Harford Moor.
         LEFT LAKE.
         PILES BROOK.
         BUTTER BROOK.

YEALM :—BLEDGABROOK.
         BROADALL LAKE.
         RED-A-VAIN.

      TORRY BROOK :—WOTTER BROOK.

Falls into the Plym at Longbridge below Plympton.

PLYM— CALVES LAKE.
         LANGCOMBE BROOK.
         SHAVERCOMBE BROOK.
         HEN TOR BROOK.
         SPANISH LAKE.
         LEGGIS LAKE.
         BLACKABROOK.

The Plym is called by some writers, in a part of its course, the Cad.

      MEAVY or MEW—Har Tor Brook.
                 Newleycombe Lake.
                 Narrator Brook.
                 Sheeps Tor Brook.
                 Lovaton Brook.

The Meavy joins the Plym at Shaugh Bridge.

WALKHAM—Spriddle Lake.
>Long Ash Brook.
The Walkham falls into the Tavy off the moor.

TAVY :—RATTLE BROOK.
>OUTER RED LAKE,
>HOMER RED LAKE. called Wester Red Lake in the Perambulation of 1609.
>BAGGA TOR BROOK.
>WILSWORTHY BROOK.
>YOULDEN BROOK.
>PETER TAVY BROOK.
>LYD—Doe Tor Brook.
>>Wallabrook.
>The Lyd falls into the Tamar.
>WEST OCKMENT—Brim Brook.
>>Red-a-vain.
Unites with the East Ockment off the moor, and falls into the Taw.
>EAST OCKMENT—Black-a-vain.
>>Moor Brook.
Its upper part is sometimes called the Skid.

TAW :—SMALL BROOK.
>BLACKATON BROOK, } Fall into the Teign off the moor.
>FORDER BROOK,

TEIGN :—NORTH TEIGN—Manger Brook.
>>Wallabrook.
>SOUTH TEIGN—Metherell Brook.
North Teign unites with South Teign just after leaving the moor.
>>HURSTON, OR HUSSON, WATER, falls into the Bovey off the moor.
>>BOVEY, falls into the Teign off the moor.
>>BECCA BROOK, falls into the Bovey. } These streams rise to the east of Widecombe Valley.
>>SIG, falls into the Lemon off the moor.
>>LANGWORTHY BROOK, falls into the Sig.
>>YEO, falls into the Dart below Ashburton.
>>RUDDYCLEAVE WATER, falls into the Dart in Buckland Woods.
>>WEBBURN—East Webburn, anciently called the Niprell.
>>>West Weburn—Grims Lake.
>>>>Bradford Brook.
The Webburn falls into the Dart below Newbridge.

SITUATION AND EXTENT OF DARTMOOR, WITH THE BOUNDS
OF THE FOREST & CHARTER OF KING JOHN.

SIR Edward Smirke, the learned antiquary, who furnished the interesting observations on the historical documents relating to Dartmoor, supplied by Mr. Pitman Jones of Exeter to the Rev. Samuel Rowe, and which appear in the Appendix to that gentleman's valuable work on the moor, in referring to the Domesday Survey, says "A tract of land, like Dartmoor, was under no circumstances likely to find its way into the enumeration of lands in Domesday, for it is very evident that the land intended to be included in it, and to which alone the description of *hides* and *carrucates* can strictly apply, was land under tillage, or some other form of profitable management, yielding an annual revenue to its owner, and therefore the fit subject of a land-tax."

Lydford, in which parish it has already been mentioned (*page* XI.) the whole of the forest of Dartmoor lies, is named in the Survey of the Conqueror, but as Sir Edward remarks, "it is clear that nothing but the *borough* * is

---

* Lydford village is now but a small one.   This is what Risdon, in his *Survey of Devon*, says of it, however.   "Doubtless, in the Saxon's heptarchy, it was a town of some note, that felt the furious rage of the merciless Danes."

there noticed." The entry relating to it is as follows : " The king has a borough Lideforde. King Edward held it in demesne. There are twenty-eight burgesses within the borough and forty-one without. Among them all they render to the king sixty shillings by weight, and they have two carucates of land without the borough. There are forty houses lying waste there since the king came into England. If an expedition goes by land or by sea it [*the borough*] renders as much service as Barnstaple or Totnes."

The parish of Lydford is situated in South Devonshire, and the village lies on the verge of the moor, the following small towns and villages also being on its borders. In a northerly direction Bridestowe comes next to Lydford, then Sourton, and Okehampton which is placed on its extreme northern edge. Proceeding in an easterly direction Belstone and Sticklepath come next, then Throwleigh, Gidleigh, and Chagford. Moreton Hampstead, Lustleigh, Bovey, Ilsington, Ashburton, Holne, Buckfastleigh, Dean, Brent and Ugborough follow, then Ivybridge, where the southermost point is reached. Cornwood comes next, and then Lutton, Sparkwell, Plympton, Shaugh, Meavy, Sheepstor and Walkhampton. Next in order follow Sampford Spiney, Whitchurch, Tavistock, Peter Tavy and Mary Tavy, which last two places are within a few miles of Lydford.

The distances across the moor " as the crow flies " are as follow, but it must not be forgotten that the conformation of the country would lengthen them to the pedestrian in no small degree.

From the Western Beacon, above Ivybridge, on the south, to Okehampton Park, on the north, rather over 22 miles—extreme length of
Dartmoor.

From borders of moor near Bridestowe to Gidleigh, about 8 miles.

From borders of moor near Lydford to Metherell, near Chagford,
about 9 miles.

From Black Down to Ilsington, about 17 miles—extreme breadth of
Dartmoor.

From borders of moor near Whitchurch to Buckland Beacon, about
13 miles.

From Sheepstor to Holne, about 9 miles.

From Shaugh to Shipley Bridge, near Brent, about 8 miles.

Average breadth of the moor, about 10 or 12 miles.

As the perambulation of the forest has several times
been referred to in the foregoing pages it may be
interesting to the reader if we give here the "boundes
and limitts" as set forth by the twenty-five jurors
who were sworn to enquire into the same, and made
their return at a Court of Survey, at Okehampton, in 1609.
There have been perambulations of Dartmoor in various
reigns; it is stated that a copy of the return to one of these
made in the time of the Conqueror exists in the Duchy
Office, and according to Mr. G. W. Ormerod, a Saxon perambulation supposed to be of the ninth century, exists
amongst the muniments of Exeter Cathedral. The record
of the perambulation of 1240, is extremely interesting and
valuable, but is not so full as the one of 1609.*

---

* Copies of the perambulation may be seen in Risdon's *Survey of Devon*,
in Westcote's *View of Devon in 1630*, in Rowe's work on the moor, and in
the papers by Mr. Spence Bate and Mr. R. Dymond in the *Transactions
of the Devonshire Association.*

Cosdon.—Hound Tor.—Waterdon Tor.—Wotesbrooke-lake foote (Wallabrook)—Hingeston, al's Highstone (The Longstone near Kes Tor) — Hethstone. — Turfehill. — King's Oven.—Wallabrook Head, "and so alonge by Wallebrooke until it fall into easter Dart, and so downwards by the said easter Dart to another Dart called wester Dart and from thence ascendinge by the said west Dart unto Wobrookefoote."—Drylake.—Dryefeild ford.—Knattle-burrow.—West Wallabrook Head, "and so by the same Wester Wellebrooke untill it falleth into Owne al's Aven" (Aune or Avon)—Eastern Whitaburrow*—Red Lake foot, "whir it falleth into Erme"—Erme Head.—Plym Head.—Eylesburrow.—Siward's Cross.—South Hisworthy Tor.—North Hisworthy Tor.—Mis Tor.—Dedlakeheadd. Luntes-borowe (Lynch Tor)—Wester Red Lake.—Rattle Brook foot, "and soe from thence to the headd of the same Rattle-brooke."—Stinka Tor—Sandy Ford, "and so from thence linyallie to the ford wch. lyeth in the east syde of the chapple of Halstocke."—Cosdon.

On *page* 85 I have mentioned that King John dis-afforested the county of Devon, with the exception of Dartmoor and Exmoor. The following is a trans-lation of the charter by which this was done, given in the fifth year of that monarch's reign, (1204) where the moor is mentioned by name.

"John by the Grace of God, King of England &c. Know ye that we have disafforested all Devon of all things

* This seems to be an error for Western Whitaburrow. Eastern Whitaburrow is not one of the forest bounds.

appertaining to the forest and foresters, unto the bounds of the ancient regards of Dertmore and Exemore, which regards were in the time of King Henry the first. So that all Devon and the men residing in it, and their heirs be altogether disafforested and acquitted, and free for us and our heirs for ever of all things appertaining to the forest and to foresters, except the two moors above named, to wit, Dertmore and Exemore by the aforesaid bounds. We will also and grant that the aforesaid men of Devon and their heirs may have the customs within the regards of those moors as they were wont to have in the time of the aforesaid King Henry, performing therefor the customs which then they were wont and ought to perform.· And that it may be lawful for them who shall please without the aforesaid bounds to essart, make parks, take all kinds of venery, to have dogs, bows and arrows and all other kinds of arms, and to make deer leaps, excepting in the limits of the aforesaid moors, where they cannot make deer leaps or hays. And if their dogs shall run into our forest we will that they be treated therefor in like manner as the other barons and knights are therefor treated who are disafforested and adjoin our forests elsewhere. And we will that one turn only of the sheriff be made by the year in the County of Devon, and that turn shall be made after the feast of Saint Michael, to enquire concerning Pleas of the Crown and other things which belong to the Crown, without hindrance made to anyone, and that he shall not make more turns unless for the attachment of Pleas of the Crown when they shall happen with the Coroners, and for assuring the peace. So, indeed, that in that Eyre he shall take nothing to his own use. And of the prisoners who shall be taken in the County of Devon whom the sheriff hath the power to bail, and whose bail the County of Devon shall be willing to take upon itself. We will and grant that by their advice they may be bailed, so that they be not any longer detained in prison through the malice or hinderance of the sheriff. And if the sheriff shall unjustly trouble the aforesaid men of Devon and he shall be convicted thereof he shall be subject to our amercement, and we will amerce him, and substitute another sheriff who will treat them well and lawfully.

Witness the Lord Herbert, Bishop of Salisbury; Geoffrey Fitz Peter, Earl of Essex; Baldwin, Earl of Albemarle; William, Earl Ferrars; Henry, Earl of Hereford; William de Braosa. Given by the hand of the Lord S. Elect of Chichester, at Winchester, on the eighteenth day of May, in the fifth year of our reign."

NOTE.—Since the foregoing chapters were written the Clapper Bridge at Dartmeet, referred to on pages 18, 84, has been re-erected by the Dartmoor Preservation Association.

FINIS.

INDEX.

ERRATA.

Page 45, line 3, for " Fur Tor " read " Cut Hill."
Poge 117, line 22, for " North-west " read " North-east."
Pags 139, line 7, omit " and which at first quite startled me.

ILLUSTRATIONS.

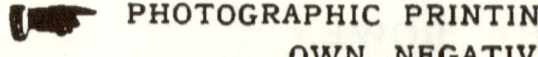

The Lockyer Hotel,

(Late Harvey's),

LOCKYER St., PLYMOUTH.

THIS first-class **Family Hotel** having been thoroughly renovated and refurnished, will be found replete with every comfort, combined with moderate charges.

Visitors and Tourists will find it pleasantly situated within a few minutes walk of the Great Western Railway Station, the Millbay Docks, and the Hoe, and close to the Athenæum, Theatre, and Tram Terminus.

The Cuisine receives careful attention.

COFFIN & HOLMES,

Proprietors.

W. H. LUKE,

Bookseller, Stationer & Printer,

ILLUMINATOR & ENGRAVER,

8, Bedford Street, PLYMOUTH.

—PUBLISHER OF THE—

HISTORY OF PLYMOUTH

BY LLEWELLYN JEWITT.

With Illustrations, Maps, &c.   Price, Demy 8vo. 21/-;
Demy 4to., 30/-.

Handbook of Plymouth, Devonport & Stonehouse

BY W. H. K. WRIGHT, F.R.H.S.

With Illustrations and Maps.   Price 1/-, by post 1/3.

PHOTOGRAPHIC VIEWS OF PLYMOUTH AND NEIGHBOURHOOD.

A very Large Series to select from.   **From SIXPENCE EACH.**

THE ROYAL CABINET ALBUM OF VIEWS
OF PLYMOUTH & NEIGHBOURHOOD.

18 VIEWS, IN CLOTH.   PRICE 1/-, BY POST 1/2.

Maynard & Son,

ARMY & HUNTING

SADDLERS.

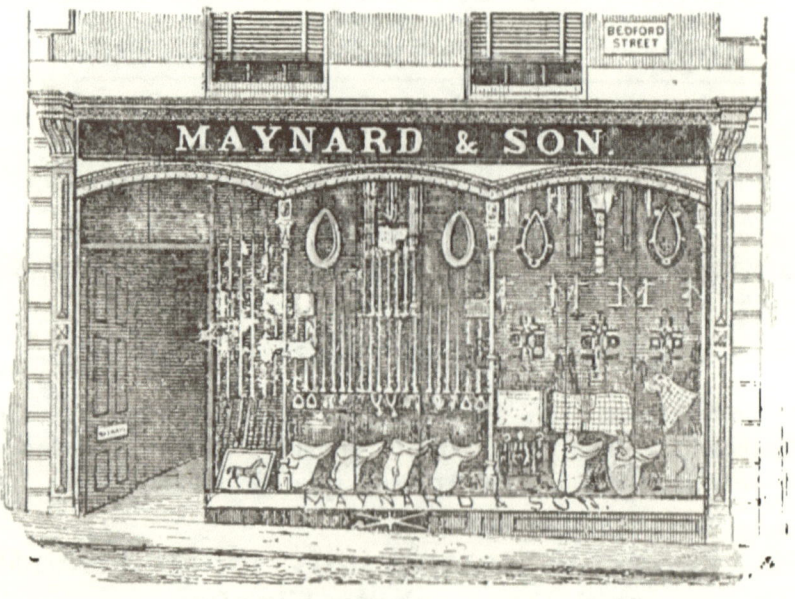

BEDFORD STREET,

Plymouth.

BY THE SAME AUTHOR;

With Map and numerous Illustrations, Octavo, Cloth—Price 4/6.

THE

Ancient Crosses of Dartmoor;

With a Description of their Surroundings.

❖ Opinions of the Press. ❖

—:o:—

MR. CROSSING has done his work most conscientiously and thoroughly, and has said almost all that can be said about Dartmoor crosses *Saturday Review.*

A book about Dartmoor, written by a competent hand, giving an accurate account of some of its notable relics—*Western Times.*

This is a useful guide to the crosses which still remain on Dartmoor. MR. CROSSING is, of course, aware of their religious signification and uses, but he has come to the conclusion—indeed, we think we may say, demonstrated—that many of the Dartmoor crosses were also boundary marks and guides by which the wanderer might be helped in finding his way in that trackless wild - *Notes and Queries.*

MR. CROSSING is an enthusiastic lover of Dartmoor; and although the main interest of the work he has just produced lies in its antiquarian and historical features there is not wanting abundant evidence that the beauty and poetry of Dartmoor scenery as they appeal to the eye and the soul of the artist touch responsive chords in the breast of the man who has written these pages—*Western Daily Mercury.*

MR. CROSSING evidently knows the moor intimately, and has gathered many a legend and wonder-story from its older inhabitants. **** The descriptions of the natural features of the moor in the different seasons are not the least charming part of the book—*Literary World.*

Carefully prepared, well-written, and effectively illustrated—*Western Morning News.*

Must form a welcome addition to any library—*Western Guardian.*

MR. CROSSING'S book will not only be invaluable to the antiquary, but will, no doubt, be much sought for by the tourist on the moor who desires to know something more of these memorials of bye-gone ages, than can be gathered from the peasantry living in the neighbourhood—*Torquay Directory.*

The lover of antiquities will delight in the pages of this work. It abounds with information the most exact, and is the result of explorations extending over many years—*Weekly Express.*

The author has evidently written the book *con amore*, and has interspersed the descriptions and histories of the various crosses which are to be found in the wilds of Devonshire, with pleasant word pictures of the moorland scenery—*Western Figaro.*

No better authority than MR. CROSSING could possibly be found to deal with this interesting subject, for the author has a most intimate acquaintance with Dartmoor—*Western Antiquary.*

MR. CROSSING has not only rescued the crosses from oblivion, but he has imparted to each a history, and to some a positive halo—*Tavistock Gazette.*

MR. CROSSING concludes an interesting account by a record of work done by the Dartmoor Preservation Association—*Evening Express.*

The work is well bound, is printed on good paper, and contains a map of Dartmoor, ten lithographic plates, and a useful index—*Devon Weekly Times.*

LONDON :—C. ELKIN MATHEWS.

EXETER :— J. G. COMMIN. AND ALL BOOKSELLERS.

www.ingramcontent.com/pod-product-compliance
Lightning Source LLC
Chambersburg PA
CBHW030645030726
47497CB00006B/1962